INTERVIE

Skills and St......gy

The Author

It is the convention, in books and courses or conferences, to give the audience a potted biography of the author or speaker. All too often this is a precis of a CV which would not tempt you to hire him or her and certainly does not address the question of their authority to pontificate on the subject in hand. The following brief extracts may go some way to demonstrate this author's relevance:

- John Courtis has over thirty years' work experience, in the accountancy profession, RAF, manufacturing industry (with Ford and Deeko) and recruitment, with a total of twenty years in Reed Executive, Executive Appointments and John Courtis and Partners
- he has therefore been interviewed by a wide variety of professionals, and others, when he was still an employee
- he has also spent twenty years interviewing other people and recognizes there is still room for improvement
- as a consultant, he has suffered at second hand when his clients misused the interview process; as every mistake costs him time or money, he has tended to notice and record the malpractices
- he has been active in management education for the Institute of Personnel Management, the Institute of Chartered Accountants, the Recruitment Society and the recruitment trade association (the Federation of Recruitment and Employment Services), of which he is a past Chairman
- he is almost certainly the only selection consultant to have become Chairman of a client PLC on the strength of his recruitment work
- he has over a dozen books in print on management and related subjects, for several publishers, most of whom had a free choice.

This format has the further merit that you do not have to read about the author's hobbies, family, education, marksmanship, prizes, politics, religion, decorations and former titles; you can just get on with the book.

INTERVIEWS:
Skills and Strategy

John Courtis

Cartoons by Joe Stockton

Institute of Personnel Management

First published 1988
Reprinted 1989

Phototypeset by James Jenkins Typesetting (Wandsworth)
and printed in Great Britain by Dotesios Printers Ltd.
Bradford-on-Avon, Wiltshire.

British Library Cataloguing in Publication Data
Courtis, John
    Interviews
    1. Personnel. Interviewing – Manuals
    I. Title
    658.3'1124

ISBN 0-85292-406-2

Contents

Plagiarism

This is the section normally called Acknowledgements in less forthright books. The author wishes to acknowledge that most writing is based upon a process of accidental or deliberate plagiarism, usually of work which is only dimly remembered and therefore cannot be the subject of a formal acknowledgement. This work is no different, in that it has been influenced by nearly everyone the author has been observing at work, listening to or reading (on interviewing and related subjects) over a very long period. He has read a lot of Drucker, Parkinson, Townsend, Galbraith, various Stewarts and a little Boulestin. Relevant input has also come from G.K. Chesterton, Conan Doyle and Emma Lathen.

However, he also wishes to point out that he has spent much time thinking about the subject and is of the opinion that there may be several wholly new ideas lurking in the following pages. If you come across one that seems unfamiliar, there is some possibility that it falls in this category and the author is willing to take credit for it, while waiting hopefully for the ultimate accolade – that it is rapidly plagiarized.

Conventional acknowledgements are due to several industrial and occupational psychologists, particularly D. Mackenzie Davey, Andrew Stewart and Kate Keenan. The other convention is that one's colleagues and family are thanked for being helpful and tolerant during the creation of the book. This is necessary, as the author was more than usually difficult during the latter weeks.

Finally, instead of thanking the typist, the author has to acknowledge that he put the thing together on a typewriter (albeit electronic) because he couldn't master the word-processing program on his PC in time; there must therefore be an unsung hero at the IPM who will have had to spot rather more typos than usual. His name is Matthew Reisz.

Foreword

Who should read this? This book is for everyone who has to interview people for recruitment and selection purposes, including all personnel managers, most other managers (staff and line), selection and search consultants, employment agency staff and even members of professions which often forget to practice management!

Why bother? Businesses run on money and people. Better recruitment can yield better people. The interview is the most crucial (and defective) part of the recruitment process. The nature and quality of the questions asked are an important and neglected part of that process. Correctly planned, they can save time and improve the 'filter'. Badly or unplanned, they can

- permit the recruitment of unsatisfactory employees
- allow you to miss good ones, or
- demotivate people you want to hire so that they decline your offer of employment.

How to use it. Before you reach the happy stage at which you apply all the lessons of this book from use and familiarity, there is going to be an interim period while you accept the principles involved but cannot apply the detail from memory. In the early stages you may find it necessary to do a manuscript transcript of the questions you feel relevant to each interview. Later, a brief algorithm with key words in the little boxes should suffice.

Some form of preparation is the key. We shall explore later the extent to which better preparation for the interview as a whole can also have a favourable impact on the results. One quote may be appropriate. In 1985 the Industrial Society did a survey on the quality of interviewing in British industry. It concluded that 'Poor interviews are costing millions of pounds every year.' You can do better.

Finally, it must be realized that this sort of book cannot be encyclopaedic. Although there is a case for using some of the sample questions verbatim, they are only examples and it is possible to apply the principles while using words you are happier with. There are very good reasons why, in courts, the phrase 'Tell me in your own words' seems to recur. The result is usually more natural and the resultant communication usually better.

No matter what the context, appraisal, recruitment, even audit, do first each day the thing you least want to do, because it will be the most important

Introduction

This book is largely about interviews in the recruitment process, but the core content applies to all fact-finding interviews as well as interviews used for counselling, discipline and appraisal. To hire and keep people, you can use interviews in several ways. We shall explore the need for the interview, the objectives, how to interview better, how to complement them, rely on them less and perhaps avoid them. From the reservation implied above, you can deduce that this book is not in praise of interviews. On the contrary, we shall proceed from the assumption that most interviews are unsatisfactory in some respect. Users – i.e. those who do the interviews rather than their victims – compound the problem by accepting both that the interview is necessary and that it is a satisfactory tool. On the other hand, most personnel managers have grave reservations about the quality of the interviews conducted by those around them in most organizations. Defective hiring interviews, dismissals, warning meetings and in some cases even interviews intended to record favourable appraisals have all been misunderstood by the victims in recent years to such an extent that they lead to industrial tribunals.

The objective in most interviews is a better-run organization which can be more efficient and profitable via better people-handling. Interviewers in general are likely to be aware of the objective but fail to relate their planning and conduct of the interview closely enough to this context. This complacency means that the results of the interview are frequently less than adequate. This can generate failure to hire the right people, demotivated existing staff, litigation, loss of people who could have been useful employees and in many cases distress for all involved.

There are solutions. What follows includes ways to improve the interview and some alternatives.

En route to your objective, which undoubtedly ought to benefit the organization, we can offer you certain additional benefits, most but not all of them contributing to the corporate weal. The following come to mind:

- better use of management time

- happier employees

- a better image for the organization, in the eyes of all it interviews and many it chooses not to

- more people in the right jobs, less or none in the wrong ones

- better teams within the organization

- applying the techniques recommended for improved questioning in the interview to other face-to-face encounters at work can improve communication and performance throughout an organization

- applying the thinking processes recommended can turn you from average – or good – towards brilliance!

- understanding body language and the messages of tests can help you manage people better

- test results can help you promote and develop people better

- understanding the defects of the interview can help you cure, or allow for, your colleagues' failures in this area

- improving the pre-interview processes, including sourcing, can generate instant expense savings

- some headcount savings may also be possible

- avoiding unnecessary interviews, either by eliminating candidates altogether or by using alternative filters, can also produce instant savings

- a reputation for excellence, personal and corporate, may also result. Imagine the advantage of always having the good candidates turn up for interview reliably because of your reputation for effective interviewing!

The list is not endless, but you may be able to add a few more items after reading the book.

Finally, it may be helpful to demonstrate why the interview is still so well accepted, in spite of the expert opinions against it. If we take the recruitment interview as the prime example, users may be content with the results for a variety of reasons which have nothing to do with its effectiveness as a predictor of work performance. This may be because:

- the interview was actually being used to test personal chemistry rather than performance
- the candidate correctly assessed that he or she was right for the job and sold well enough to get it
- the interview was actually being used to gather enough data to permit a 'scored biodata' exercise
- other filters, complementary to the interview, were the main basis of assessment
- the interview was unnecessary as a filter because almost anybody meeting the minimum advertised criteria could do the job tolerably well
- all parties involved wanted to believe in the interview, for one or more of the above reasons
- the interviewer was satisfied with the results; although the candidate was not, he or she was inhibited from saying so or doing anything about it; this is often the case both for those who are successful and those who are rejected.

All of these combine to perpetuate the dominance of the interview as a basis of assessment, when objective post-audit suggests that only a tiny minority of interviews really perform this function. Armed with a healthy cynicism based on these revelations, you are now equipped to tackle the corrective action necessary and to convince the hordes around you that there actually is some scope for improvement. If they need any further examples, point to the selection world, where alleged professionals, selling their powers of assessment by interview to an expectant public, have a disastrous record when it comes to recruiting for their own teams . . .

What is an Interview?

The various dictionary definitions come together in a core view that an interview is a meeting between two or more people, with an objective. Dictionary definitions are not ideal in the real world, but this is an adequate start. In several ways it points to a better context for the interview:

- there are cases where it would be politic to call the event a meeting rather than an interview; to some people, meetings sound less threatening

- not only should there be an objective, it should be known to both (or all) parties, to avoid the risk that anyone is present for the wrong purpose, or none

- in this high-tech age, a face-to-face meeting may be replaced by long-distance audio-visual contact on a private television link. This has certain disadvantages but comes within the scope of this text. It is also a useful reminder that interviews happen in places other than offices. Even if you do not appear on Wogan, you can choose to meet in hotel lounges, pubs, parks, car parks, restaurants or on the golf course. Some of these may be expedient rather than adopted by choice, but they can improve the quality of communication by relaxing one or more of the participants.

.... you can choose to meet in car parks

THE CURRENT CONTEXT

*UK managers
as interviewers
are
amateur,
disorganized,
hit and miss,
inflexible,
soft and careless*

Gut Feel

One of the major barriers to a proper understanding of the defects of the interview is the vast band of people who make interview decisions on 'gut feel', often within minutes of starting the meeting. You can probably appreciate how inexpressibly irritating this is to a recruiter or any other personnel professional who is trying to introduce a degree of objectivity into the selection process.

The author had an interesting example of this with one client who freely confessed to being a one-minute recruiter in this fashion, but also confessed that he knew it was wrong – yet it worked, for his team. He was also willing to debate why it worked, which was useful because it looked like being a significant problem for anyone trying to help him recruit. On enquiry, it turned out that he and his colleagues also set great store by a good academic record, other evidence of a high IQ, the candidates' interest in their odd but demanding company and a CV with some evidence of initiative and excellence.

After some discussion, the diagnosis was simple. They were not using the interview as an interview. It was only being used as a filter to check on personal chemistry with the existing team or to ratify reservations about the CV. The real filters were at the earlier stages and could be roughly described as an informal but thorough version of 'scored biodata', together with a degree of disclosure to (very intelligent) candidates which permitted them a degree of self-selection.

There is a happy ending. Once the value of the interview had been relegated to its proper, lesser, place we were able to discuss what other filters could be introduced to speed and refine the process, bringing to interview some people who might otherwise have been missed and avoiding interviews with people where the 'gut feel' rejection was correct but could have been achieved without the time spent on an interview. In this context it is worth considering, for certain levels of employee, tests which can be used before or instead of the interview.

Subjective Discrimination

It might get tedious to repeat the statutory and good practice constraints which affect the conduct of the interview. Instead, it may be helpful to recognize that some of your colleagues could be practising more subjective forms of bias. You need to be aware of them so that you can eliminate them or at least vaccinate the offenders against their worst traits.
For instance:

- there are people who won't hire short men
- others who rely more on star signs than on the conduct of the interview
- those who won't recruit the ugly
- others who are prejudiced against beards
- managers who will not hire people who live alone, no matter what their alleged marital state, because they have no sheet anchor/sounding board
- dog lovers who dislike cat fanciers – and vice versa
- men with 'unmanly' hobbies and women with manly ones may be suspect
- fat people and anorexics are assumed to have personality problems
- those who habitually wear suede shoes also attract adverse views
- Finally, it is possible to find those who actively dislike certain types of moustache, monocles, mean mouths, eyes too close together, 'Scargill' haircuts (baldness hidden by hair trained from one side), scruffy dress, certain accents, dirty shoes, odd spectacle frames, funny hats and bow ties.

Given this broad spectrum of bias, the wonder is that any interview can be successful, not least because some of these subjective whims are unknown to their owners. Others, who know their views are biased, justify their position much as insurance underwriters justify discriminatory premiums, by quoting past adverse 'claims experience'.

This raises an intriguing point. There are well-accepted indicators which, in combination, suggest a vulnerability to illness or to psychological problems. Is the employer justified in taking account of them? Or in trying to find out about them? Provided it does not breach current employment legislation, the answer must be 'Yes' and application forms must change accordingly.

Emotional Barriers

There are very good reasons why interviews are done badly, apart from those outlined in the Introduction. They are in general human rather than managerial ones. Think about your own organizations past and present and all classes of interview, from hiring through to termination. It is likely that you will have encountered some or all of these:

- most people do not like interviewing
- most are to some degree uncomfortable about the process
- many talk too much
- some don't talk too much but have not learned the art of listening
- many do not encourage communication because they do not wish to embarrass the interviewees
- some cannot control the interviewees
- a few regard the interview as an ego trip

All of these human failings are understandable, although not necessarily forgivable if you are the victim – or if your work and objectives suffer at second hand. However, there is worse to come. Several studies in the last few years have produced

Interviewers habitually do the things they're good at during an interview, not the things that are most needed.

more specific complaints about the conduct of interviews. The IPM, the Industrial Society and a few outplacement consultancies have looked at current practice and been appalled by what they found. CEPEC (the Centre for Professional and Educational Counselling), in a study by Dr Tony Lake in 1985, said that UK managers were amateur, disorganized, hit and miss, inflexible, soft and careless.

The other critics mentioned, inter alia, that interviews were often:

- unplanned (specifically, the interviewers had no idea what questions they were going to ask)
- devoid of two-way communication
- lacking a clear context (some people thought they were being counselled when in fact they were being given a formal warning!)
- unstructured (giving the impression that instead of following a mental algorithm the interviewers were making up the structure as they went along; 'woolly' was the kindest adjective applied by the victims)
- subjective
- gratuitously stressful
- unrecorded
- recorded without reference to specific criteria
- administered by untrained interviewers
- administered by people glaringly devoid of interpersonal skills
- boring
- ineffective as a demonstration of the organization's merits or consideration for people
- repetitive (too many interviews include massive duplication of content and, as a natural consequence, massive omissions!)
- inefficient, because so much time had to be spent correcting errors or omissions in the pre-interview processes

- administered by people who were not properly briefed, not interested, tired, drunk possessed of hidden agendas, unfamiliar with current anti-discrimination codes and, in several cases,

- unaware of the identity of the interviewee!

This catalogue may bring a wry smile to many seasoned personnel practitioners or indeed weathered managers in other functions, because some of the examples are close to home.

Unfortunately, every example damages not only the immediate exercise, whether recruitment, dismissal, counselling or appraisal, but also the organization's relationship with employees and potential employees. Worse, even those who are discounted because they are not perceived as potential employees in the immediate context may be tomorrow's recruits, customers, suppliers or just corporate friends. Bad interview practice demotivates them on some or all fronts.

The damage to the current exercise, by the way, apart from ruining the constructive effects of a counselling or appraisal session, may render a warning process invalid in law and deprive it of any remedial effect. On the recruitment front, the errors and omissions can cause late, costly, bad or non-existent hirings.

Given this catholic range of potential ills, it is not enough to say that one can measure the effectiveness of any interviewing exercise by its results. The narrow results may be perceived as successful while the side effects erode or outweight the primary result. The nearest parallel from an older profession is 'The operation was a success, but the patient died.'

Similarly, it is not enough to conduct and conclude an interview if the context is wrong. Some interviewers regard an interview as a device for assessing what is wrong with the candidate; the moment they find and can record a good reason for rejection they record it and close the meeting quickly. This is bad for two reasons. It sets a bad example and it results in an incomplete assessment of the individual, who might in fact be marginal for the current vacancy (so that you need to reconsider him or her later, when desperate) and relevant for something in the future. In both cases, the interview has failed in its purpose.

The brief for all recruitment interviews – reinforced by the layout of the assessment forms which *all* interviewers, at all levels, ought to complete – should be a context in which the interviewers are deciding *how* the candidates would perform in the job, not just making a Yes/No decision about their acceptability. It is not unknown for interviewers to reject people on personal criteria not present in the candidate specification and indeed irrelevant to the job in question.

Forcing the negative interviewers to report properly, so that an unsupported or unrelated rejection becomes unacceptable behaviour requires persuasion, education or massive authority, but it pays dividends.

Accentuate the positive, as the song has it.

The interview and indeed the whole recruitment process should identify how well the candidate would do the job, not just produce reasons for avoiding the question . . .

Avoiding Gratuitous Error

All this stress on bad practice has a purpose: to demonstrate that in the attempt to achieve best practice in anything, you do not necessarily start from zero or a neutral position. There are many colleagues occupying a minus position. Two examples may help. The Managerial Grid of Dr Blake and Dr Mouton scores managers on two scales representing people-orientation and results-orientation. Unfortunately both scales are given only positive values, so you can be anything from 0.0 to 9.9 or, more probably, 0.9 and 9.0. In the real world, we have to recognize the existence of the Bad Managers Grid, which includes a similar range of negative values, thus accepting that there are people, some of them working near you, who can produce minus scores on either axis or on both. Sales staff obsessed with turnover rather than profit are classic examples on the results axis, managers dedicated to harassing subordinates, sexually or otherwise, score negatively on the people axis. If you are to understand the process of interviewing well, it is therefore important to understand the existence of bad interviewing. There is a strong possibility, approximating to a certainty, that someone who works near you does not fully avoid gratuitous error in the recruitment process, or the pre- and post-interview stages.

If the pre-interview process is not properly carried out, several unhappy consequences inevitably emerge. For instance, if it is assumed that every departure leaves a vacancy which has to be filled, there are at least three possible problems:

(a) someone is recruited who soon perceives that the job is a non-job and leaves

(b) worse, you recruit someone who does *not* perceive this, or chooses to ignore the fact, and stays

(c) you and your colleagues perceive this after wasting a lot of time and money on the recruitment exercise.

In extreme cases there are two other possibilities:

Most management errors are
errors of omission particularly
in communication. Not listening
may be the main offence

'Do tell me a little about yourself.'

(d) you recruit a permanent employee for a temporary need

(e) you recruit when you ought to promote or reallocate duties.

Good job analysis should prevent this. It should also prevent a situation in which the need has not been defined clearly, or at all, and agreed by all parties. This is depressingly common. The conventional errors include:

(a) failure to do any job analysis

(b) defining the ideal candidate without considering what minimum criteria would be acceptable

(c) failure to agree the specification, so that the various decision makers are looking for different people – or largely the same ones but with a hidden agenda in somebody's mind

(d) failure to consider whether the job will appeal to the sort of candidates specified

(e) failure to consider whether the candidates specified are available for the rewards package (not just salary) you have in mind.

All the good interviewing skills in town will not dig you out of a disaster area ravaged by one or more of these.

Imprecision at the analysis stage also has a deleterious effect on the resourcing. If your definition of the candidate is wrong, the choice of source and everything associated with it can be affected, and the flow to the interview process inhibited. For instance, until you know how wide or narrow your choice is, you do not know whether you can undertake a slim low-budget exercise with ruthless criteria, or you need maximum effort and a willingness to accept the only candidate who meets your minimum requirements. If you get the balance wrong, you may recruit late, badly, not at all – or well, but at unnecessary expense.

The errors which can be made in resourcing are manifold. The choice of sources includes any of the following, alone or in combination:

(a) advertising
(b) agencies or registers, including Job Centres and the PER
(c) selection consultants

(d) headhunters
(e) a do-it-yourself headhunt
(f) outplacement consultants.

The wrong source gets chosen because employers fail to realize how desperate their situation is, but the later interview process gets fouled up at this point. Take a case in which direct advertising has been chosen; all the following mistakes are possible, and more:

(a) as already indicated, the wrong candidate specification can lead to the wrong choice of media and an inadequate or irrelevant response

(b) if the basic disclosure rules as to
   • salary package
   • location
   • company description
   • job title and content
   • candidate requirements
   • and sympathetic reply instructions

are ignored, you may write an ad which, at a stroke, repels the right candidates, attracts the wrong ones and leaves every reader with a sense of your corporate incompetence.

From this point on, everything that is done wrong loses good candidates and keeps bad ones in play. The things frequently done wrong before, during and after the recruitment interview include:

• failing to provide adequate data before the interview, so that candidates (unless they are very desperate) withdraw as soon as they fully understand what the job is

• unsympathetic interview times

• failing to double-check if interview appointments are not confirmed – no postal service is perfect

• excessively extending an interview programme so the people you saw first get bored before you finish seeing the rest

• subjective interview techniques

• delay in making a decision after interviews

- requiring too many interviews before a decision is reached

- rejecting some candidates because they interview badly, some because they test badly and the rest because they don't meet somebody's hidden agenda.

Some of these problems cannot afflict non-recruitment interviews. Others in the list above have equivalents in other types of interview, but they may not be identified as problems because they only affect existing employees, who in most cases do not think it politic to complain and cannot afford the luxury of walking out on the process before or even during the exercise. The reverse can also be true. We recently encountered a case in which a senior manager had been fired, with infinite tact, notice and gentleness, to such an extent that he was still in post three months later, not realizing that his notice had expired. Better communication and some documentation might have avoided this.

Documentation is important. Many of the errors which mar otherwise satisfactory interviews are actually omissions. Telling people in advance what the interview is about and, where appropriate, providing background material, can speed and enhance the conduct of the interview itself. They also prevent firings being understood as formal warnings, warnings being construed as unique counselling, counselling being mistaken for a normal appraisal (or vice versa) and a promotion, in one ghastly recent case, being construed as an optional demotion!

Excellence in recruitment brings excellence in profits. If not, perhaps your objectives are muddled?

> *Are your questions probing, powerful, incisive, calculated and searching? If not, why not scrap them and develop better ones*

'Are you a crook, Mr. Lightfinger?'

The Impossible Task

In support of our contention that interviews bear an impossible burden, consider the questions the interviewers need to ask themselves. For example, at management level, these must include the following:

(a) are candidates' qualifications relevant, adequate and genuine?

(b) is their alleged experience adequate and genuine?

(c) what have they omitted from their CVs which could be significant, for or against them?

(d) how do they behave in a team? (and can they control meetings?)

(e) are they assertive?

(f) how intelligent are they, and is their IQ adequate for the job?

(g) can they manage and keep support staff and perhaps a labour force?

(h) can they motivate people?

(i) do they develop people well, if at all?

(j) is their business logic and decision-making more than just adequate for the job responsibilities?

(k) are they emotionally stable?

(l) do they communicate well in writing?

(m) do they communicate well face to face?

(n) do they communicate enough?

(o) does their communication involve enough listening?

(p) are they reliable, do they do important things on time?

(q) do they tell people who depend on them if things for which they (the candidates) are responsible cannot be done on time?

(r) is their time-management sound in other respects?

(s) do they recruit successfully? (and have they developed successors?)

(t) are they honest, with their colleagues?

(u) are they fit?

(v) what have they improved (changed, prevented, stopped, started and so on)?

(w) can they survive stress?

(x) is their effect on their peers and the organization beneficial rather than just neutral or even negative?

(y) do they remember things clearly?

(z) is their conceptual thinking adequate for them to understand the corporate objectives and their own part thereof *and* to focus their own and their department's attention on them?

All twenty-six of these points are of legitimate interest to a prospective employer. All deserve at least a few minutes' attention. Only a very well structured interview or set of interviews can cover them adequately. Few interviews are planned well enough or allocated enough time . . .

Worse, at least one key question is omitted from the above list and it deserves more than a few minutes:

'Has any one of the candidates adequate technical skills to perform properly in the functional detail of the job – and perhaps subordinates' jobs – without training?'

Very few interviews do more than scratch the surface of this question, and even then the evidence is likely to be circumstantial rather than direct.

This chilling catalogue makes the case for doing all you can, in, around and instead of the interview, to reduce dependence on it! It also suggests that the amount of time allocated to each candidate needs to be measured in hours, with very thorough discipline, both as to the structure of the various interviewers' contributions and the economical use of planned questions. To lighten the burden, let us look back at the list and determine which points are susceptible to non-interview review.

(a) qualifications: partially soluble by prior exchange of documentation or telephone approach to the institutions concerned, most of whom are pleased to help on any doubtful verifications;

(b) experience: needs critical review of CV and interview attention, but correct choice and use of referees can reduce the burden;

(c) omissions: tackle at interview only;

(d) team behaviour: a clear case for Myers-Briggs, plus discussion at interview;

(e) assertion: may be identified in a properly planned interview or by one of several psychometric tests;

(f) high IQ: best identified by test, but clear pointers can be obtained from high performance at university or even membership of Mensa. However, short of these dizzy heights, selected tests may assist, without necessarily dictating that a particular minimum IQ is essential. The application of intelligence or a large dose of common-sense and communication skills may be more to the point. Pursuing high IQ for its own sake is not always necessary or wise;

(g) people management: references are the best indicator here. Formal tests run second. Interviews may or may not work, because textbook answers may not equal textbook action. Lots of managers know about management theory, but keep it theoretical and don't notice that they ignore, delay or omit the desired action;

(h) motivation: as for people management;

(i) here the interview is paramount, unless you can get references from below . . .;

(j) logic and decision-making: tests are best, although some idea can be gleaned at interview, particularly if properly planned;

(k) emotional stability: for certainty, personality tests are a must, although signs of problems may show through with a persistent interviewer;

(l) written communication: good reply instructions in the initial advertisement and letters from the employer can provoke adequate examples of how people sell themselves, but at senior level one can always ask for examples of work which do not breach confidentiality. The rider is only to make sure that you look ethical. Most candidates delight in showing how much responsibility they have by excessive exposure of confidential data. This in turn tells you something about their likely future behaviour . . .;

(m) verbal communication: a classic area for interview assessment, provided the interviewer listens carefully and questions well. However, this is not just about how well they speak, it is about their comprehension of words *heard;* there is good test material available as part of several IQ tests. Unless it is possible to devise a demanding interview script, supplementary testing may be the best way. If relying on the interview, remember to use questions which demand a discriminating response. The slightly unclear question may be useful here;

(n) adequacy of adequacy of communication: this is not about brevity, but adequacy for work purposes, so references may be helpful. Thoughtful interview probing is also needed;

(o) listening: the ideal subject for review at interview – but the interviewer has to work doubly hard to assess it!

(p) reliability: only slightly amenable to assessment at interview (although the pre-interview process may give you some help), this is better explored by personality test and reference checking. Those who foul up the appointment timing, turn up late, don't complete required paperwork, don't read yours, including reply instructions, fail to confirm by phone when asked specifically or fail to send something you have asked for (*always* ask them to do something post-interview, as a test of both their interest and their reliability) may well be as bad, or worse, at work. Absent-minded professors are all very well in fiction. Absent-minded managers are sheer hell in real life;

(q) failsafe: tests might guide, but peer-group references are best;

(r) time management: again, the peer group or boss would be best. Tests can help. The interview can scratch the surface but, short of an indiscretion based on a total lack of appreciation of good practice, will not provide a definitive answer. The usual problem is that the culprit knows fairly well what standards he or she requires of other people, but fails to observe them personally or regards a reliable standard of failure as acceptable. Such a person may be always nearly on time, like BR; others call this 'late';

(s) recruitment and development: references may help, but this is one case where the interview is the primary route, unless the candidate has built evidence, or at any rate claims, into the CV;

(t) integrity: references and a well-planned section of the interview can both help here. Tests can also shed some light. Equivocation and devious behaviour have been singled out by testers and graphologists, in the author's experience;

(u) fitness: negative signs may emerge at a meeting and

positive ones in a CV, usually under sports and hobbies, but the acid test is a formal medical examination;

(v) achievements: the CV can guide, references may help, but this is an area where the interview is vital;

(w) stress: again, negative indicators may emerge in the CV or at interview, but a formal test must be the definitive route. References only provide a limited sample and a biased one, because you don't get an objective view of the nature of the stress or the external factors affecting the victim at the time. For example, some people can survive any amount of in-company strife, provided it isn't coupled with a domestic disaster – or vice versa;

(x) beneficial impact?: references are probably the key here. Some data may emerge at a good interview. Tests are probably of peripheral use;

(y) memory: you can test for this, formally and to some extent at interview. References are less likely to help unless the problem is gross or the memory phenomenal. Anything in between will not register the shades of grey well enough for your needs;

(z) conceptual thinking: unless fantastic, or gross, this is not going to show up well enough at interview, so formal tests are probably necessary for the people on the middle ground;

The final question, beyond (z), demands an examination, skills testing, assessment centre or equivalents. Incidentally, you will note the absence of the assessment centre from the detailed answers above, because the specific routes recommended are in many cases *part* of an assessment centre syllabus and it would be unhelpful to use the sledgehammer description for each nut.

Recent events are ancient history unless you were present. Interviewers need to be archaeologists, forensic scientists, historians or detectives to bridge this gap

'I know we need proof of her Ph.D., but did you have to invite the whole examining board?'

The Uncertainty Vacuum

Interviews of all kinds are particularly vulnerable to two very human problems. One is the 'Uncertainty Matrix', to which we shall return in a few lines. The second is that people, unless well disciplined, tend to be reactive. They react to what is evident and do not notice what is not evident. In consequence, if someone on the employer's side has a hidden agenda, matched by omissions on the interviewee's side, it is entirely possible that a subject may not come up at all. If, at an appraisal interview, both sides are determined not to talk about the employee's domestic situation, it requires a substantial degree of discipline for the interviewer(s) to raise the subject, although it may actually be a primary and temporary cause of the work problems.

A candidate's CV may omit certain vital early experience, relevant A levels or peripheral skills, because the advertisement did not give enough information, no job description exists or the candidate specification is in somebody's head. In consequence, an interviewer who has not been fully briefed can fail to elicit information which would convert the candidate from looking unacceptable on paper (to the person with the full specification in his or her head) into the only viable candidate if proper disciplines had been operated. This is one good reason for asking interviewees in any class of interview 'What have we missed, what have brevity, modesty and ignorance of the context prevented you disclosing or raising before now?' You can phrase it better according to the circumstances, but if you don't ask a question you may never get the answer.

We shall cover elsewhere the extent to which the quality of answers depends on the quality of the questions. This is the most basic area: the *absence* of a question can leave a whole raft of answers undisclosed.

Now to the 'Uncertainty Matrix', which can also be observed afflicting the work of historians, courts and mundane things like motor insurance claims files. The problem is a tendency to give the wrong weight to circumstantial, second-hand and absent evidence in preference to the first-hand or the reasonable assumption. There are several factors which contribute to this confusion:

(a) the impartiality or otherwise of the observer/decision-maker
(b) his or her status (participant, eyewitness, third party)
(c) the time elapsed since the event, interview, etc., and
(d) the nature of the event.

This last is crucial. When you are trying to make a qualitative decision about someone's past career, as a guide to future performance, much of the evidence is tenuous and circumstantial. This is often true even if the subject is an existing long-service employee. (All criticism tells you as much about the critic as it does about the subject, often more, and a historic written appraisal is no exception.) There are relatively few employees, even in general management, who leave behind hard evidence of their achievements. Architects and people whose personal names are attached to a product may be an exception, but even then there can be a team input and, come to think of it, you seldom have to interview the people whose names are on the label! You normally have the daunting task of asking yourself:

● did such and such a thing happen?
● what actually was it?
● who did it?
● what was its effect on the employee's/candidate's organization and/or customers?

As, in a thorough interview, you may have to ask some or all of these questions in relation to a number of events, ranging from the victim's exam records, through skills and experience, to profit achievements, it is strongly recommended that you consider asking, perhaps in advance, for hard evidence wherever possible. In the recruitment context, after reading a candidate's CV or application form, identify the bits which may be supported by documentary evidence and ask that this be brought to the meeting.

Many managers make claims about their contributions to sales, innovation, solvency or profitability. Take them seriously.

The good ones will be impressed. Ask if the Annual Reports or other documents of record hint at these peaks. Sometimes they will. Sometimes there is corroboration in the form of a souvenir or a gracious letter.

Many candidates claim to have passed the examinations of a professional body but not to have applied for membership – often for very good reasons like lack of money, the death of their work referees during the long haul to the final examinations, or the irrelevance of the qualification to their then jobs. A firm request for a sight of the pass certificates may save a lot of time, not least because some candidates then decide to withdraw before interview.

There are other possibilities. Where the candidates claim responsibility for the creation of a past product, system report or solo project, ask that they bring the relevant presentation; the best examples are almost invariably, unless extremely confidential, saved in a professional 'bottom drawer' and still available bearing the name of the author or team leader.

You could also ask for published articles or press cuttings; these are not absolute proof but imply responsibility and may underline a past employer's approval. Other hard evidence can include 'to whom it may concern' references or current and past organization charts.

All this may have relevance for people already in your employment. There is a tendency, touched on earlier, for people to react only to what is currently obvious. In consequence, when assessing or counselling existing employees it is easy to see them only in the roles they have held in your organization. Relatively few interviewers are as thorough about people they 'know' as they would be about the record of an external candidate (and even the latter level of enquiry might not be adequate, as we explain elsewhere). 'Old John' may be viewed as a past Company Secretary and cost-centre manager by people who do not know or have not bothered to find out that he was general manager of a major profit centre in a larger and more demanding environment overseas. The 'Temp' whom everyone takes for granted may have a degree and experience disproportionate to the way the company currently uses him or her. Proper interviews and pre-interview research will address this.

At this point, both experienced and inexperienced readers may be sucking their teeth and wondering whether all this is practicable. The author had the same reservations when he first had to interview for a living. Long experience now suggests that asking for documentary corroboration, provided the request is properly presented, is a courtesy to all parties. For instance:

(a) it implies that you are taking them seriously
(b) it saves time at interview
(c) it may avoid abortive interviews
(d) it may permit the interview to be better planned
(e) it may force candidates and employees to present themselves better
(f) it makes you look more professional than other employers
(g) it must be preferable to trying to assemble questions which give the same degree of certainty without hard evidence!

The other reason for this obsession with documentation is the 'Uncertainty Matrix', with which you can chart the crude variables for past events. On the primary axis, there are three classes of 'witness', the participants, the contemporary observers or equivalents (eyewitnesses) and the rest (i.e. everyone who wasn't there). On the other axis, chart the nature of the event: the alleged event *did* happen; something different happened; nothing happened.

Historians and interviewers are in a difficult situation. They weren't there and, without hard evidence, it is sometimes very difficult to be sure whether an event in a person's career or a company's progress happened in the way described, or at all. If, in the grand scale of things, the event left no traces, the interviewer is operating at the lowest levels of certainty. Hence the emphasis you will find elsewhere on finding contemporary referees too.

All this can save you from the journalists' disease – being more certain about events than the people who were actually there! This is actually a managerial disease too, particularly prevalent among people whose preconceptions about colleagues flow in to fill the space which would otherwise be available for new data about events. They sometimes justify this by pointing out that past behaviour is the best guide to future performance –

true, but unhelpful if you are not willing to continue observing the behaviour as it passes into history. On the same fallacious basis, Robert the Bruce could have decided that his spider was not going to bridge the small gap it failed to cross the first time he watched it; his conduct might then have been as negative as the closed minds of these managers.

Every time you reply to a candidate or other interviewee with an opinion you deprive yourself of the chance to ask a question

ALTERNATIVES AND AIDS

Interview substitutes are attractive not just because interviews are so bad but because some substitutes do not demand the presence of the candidate . . . Others do not require the presence of the interviewer

Introduction

All this emphasis on the defects of the interview is intended to condition you into considering alternatives and complementary filters. These fall into three groups. The first, very crudely, is things you can do without the candidates being present. The second includes all those things which demand the candidates' attendance. The third covers alternatives to the interview.

In the first group we find things like:

- astrology
- scored biodata
- graphology
- references
- an objective review of the way candidates sell themselves
- a self-selection process based on the data you send to them about the company and the job.

The second includes:

- assessment centres
- psychometric tests
- self-administered algorithms via computer
- palmistry
- phrenology
- medical examination
- craft or professional examinations.

The third, particularly if you are undertaking recruitment rather than selection (and are therefore prepared to hire anyone meeting the minimum criteria who actually wants the job), includes some of the above plus a briefing by audio-visual means. The only difficulty is that candidates, even if they are offered the job, may feel cheated if they do not undergo a conventional interview! It may be necessary to have someone spend time with them just to provide the illusion of an interview, although the actual decision is being made on other criteria! This also permits the line boss to ensure that personal chemistry is not too wildly out.

The following sections explore these additional filters in more detail.

Alternatives within Interviews

There is one encouraging feature about the relative merits of work samples, ability tests, assessment centres and scored biodata as against the average interview – that you can steal ideas from these highly rated alternatives to enhance your own and your colleagues' interview performance.

All four of the alternatives mentioned have an effectiveness as predictors several times as great as normal interviews. The art is to run something better than normal. We explore elsewhere (page 60) how 'scored biodata' can be integrated into the interview and pre-interview process, but it may seem a little far-fetched that interviews could incorporate assessment-centre concepts, tests and work-sample exercises. Not so. The interview already incorporates several features which generate the same kind of answers as work samples:

- can the candidates concentrate on what you are saying?
- do they understand complex questions?
- do they understand simple ones?
- can they give concise, intelligible, yet full answers to reasonable questions?
- do they understand the technical words you are using, which are necessary in the vacancy under discussion?
- do they fully understand the words they are using?
- if you outline a recent practical or conceptual problem, giving them adequate background data, is their approach to the problem logical? (This may be more important than their suggested solutions!)

All the above offer samples of the way people will perform at work, provided that the questions are clear and audible. In fact, it can be argued that people are more likely to concentrate at interview than in the work situation, which should balance out against the problem of interview nerves. If the interviewer's noting and analysis are satisfactory, concentration on these points can offer above-average prediction of these aspects of performance. Further thought can offer more parallels.

Body Language

Studying body language, or non-verbal signals, is a tricky business. Like appraisal, it might be safer not to do it than to do it inadequately. Equally, it is not possible to cover it adequately in a small slice of this book. Read one of the specialist books on the subject if you want to go further, but in the meantime we offer a caveat and an opportunity. The caveat is that you should not rely on partial knowledge of the subject. Remembering a few key signals and attempting to draw conclusions when they crop up is extremely dangerous, primarily because groups of signals rather than lone examples seem to be more reliable. In any case, apart from identifying that someone is lying, the information you get is peripheral rather than direct.

There is an exception, which constitutes the opportunity. Do take the trouble to learn the signs of interest and of boredom so that you can encourage interviewees as appropriate and avoid putting them off at a crucial point by a genuine but tactless signal – or a misplaced one. A few gracious gestures, leaning forward, making eye contact, nodding, smiling and giving little interested noises all help. Arranging a clock behind the interviewee so you can see it out of the corner of your eye without losing eye contact – assuming good eyesight and large hands (on the clock) – can also avoid the pressure generated by glancing at your watch. If you have forgotten the clock set-up, look at the interviewee's watch when the opportunity offers itself – this is much less obvious.

It also gives comfort if you mirror the interviewee's stance discreetly. If overdone, this tends to get a bit like synchronized swimming and will be noticed, but if you drift towards each new position it will give reinforcement to your image. A natural bit of role-playing, even if it is noticed, is likely to be favourably interpreted. Role-playing is important, quite apart from the body language involved. If you are being professional about your interviewing, this implies projecting interest, competence, communication, assertion and a degree of omniscience. Interviewers are not supposed to bring the problems of the previous hour, or week, into the interview. Act well. Better interviews will result.

Take the trouble to learn the signs of interest and boredom...

Artificial Aids

In most recruitment exercises the interviewers spend a substantial minority of the allotted interview time briefing the candidates about the job. Even if they have sent a written brief in advance, there is still a need to add detail and run the candidate in with background material.

This is in many cases a waste of time. Obviously, there must be some time allocated to a question-and-answer session on this front, but if the interviewers' time is valuable, there must be a case for mechanizing the process. This can be on several levels, depending on the sophistication of the hardware available and the volume of candidates to be processed.

At the most basic level you can give the candidates more words, pictures and numbers, on paper. Next is the possibility of the same sort of package, supplemented by an audio presentation. Next, perhaps an audio-visual presentation using slide/tape media or even a full-scale film. Better still, as television sets and video recorders are readily available, access to a video camera can permit a video presentation. This does not have to be elaborate; in fact a home movie of the person who is later going to carry out the interview can give a sense of continuity and immediacy. (If you are not sure which of two or more people will do the interview, try to ensure that each has a speaking part in the presentation.)

This has several advantages. Apart from the time-saving, it ensures that each candidate receives the same preliminary brief, so that the quality of their later questions is a legitimate basis for assessing them and is not influenced by the extent to which the interviewer briefed them well or badly. Better still, it gives them a chance to get in the right frame of mind without an unfriendly audience.

Finally, if you plan to process hundreds of bodies, there may be a case for assembling a presentation which is genuinely interactive. Several firms will produce an interactive video which permits the candidate to work through a simple algorithm, depending on which bits of a heavy brief are of most interest to them or (in graduate or blue-collar recruitment) which jobs they want to sample or review in depth. This may seem somewhat impersonal, but it must be remembered that the time saved by this technique gives the interviewers *more* time per capita to do the genuinely personal bit, without having to collapse from boredom repeating, badly, a tedious catalogue of the things the package can do better.

Incidentally, buying a video camera also offers you the option of taping the interview itself, if the candidates need to be considered by staff not present on the day, either because of other pressures or because they usually work in a different country. It can also permit the interviewer to re-assess a candidate's performance without the pressure implicit in running the interview.

Do not assume that a video camera is expensive. Certainly it is possible to spend sums well into four figures (sterling), but the cheapest black-and-white models were available at less than £1000 at the time of writing. Running expenses are negligible.

On a more mundane level, consider having a Polaroid camera to hand. Relatively few interviewers have total recall of the people they have seen and if you do it after you have met rather than requiring their submission in advance, photographs cannot be regarded as having a discriminatory effect.

Depending on the nature of the jobs you have in mind, do consider exposing candidates to the hardware they are supposed to master or be familiar with, whether computer keyboard, word processor, typewriter, telephone or arc welder. It is a courtesy to the candidate, not just a skills test and may generate a product which leaves some hard evidence of their competence for later review. The people who might wrongly take you to a tribunal because of a chance remark by an inept line manager are going to find it more difficult to argue against a tape, piece of paper or dangerous weld which demonstrates how they fell short of the successful candidates.

Astrology

The author is somewhat diffident about mentioning this subject but has concluded it needs to be included, on merit. Unfortunately the merits are relatively slim. There is a considerable body of evidence available that people born under particular star signs tend to share certain personality characteristics. Limited experiments also tend to suggest that certain types of job attract an above-average density of people born under a minority of signs. The catch is that the tendency in each case, although statistically significant, is not so great as to justify the use of astrology as a predictor in selection work. On balance, if you have nothing else to go on when choosing between two identical candidates and you have established a valid pattern in specific functions in your own organization – a pattern of above-average performance, not just entry into the function – don't toss a coin, choose the preferred star sign. There are, of course, relatively few cases where all other things are equal.

Healthy cynicism may be the safer posture, since if you want to consider all the factors which make star signs so unreliable, you have to go back to first principles and think what actually causes the differences, if any. It is unlikely that the ancients' view about the positions of other planets is relevant. Much more likely, surely, is the seasonal influence upon the mother's body (weather, foods, etc.) or upon the infant in the twelve months after birth. If this is so, there must be a difference between Northern and Southern hemispheres, and indeed the Equatorial regions. Equally, premature babies may not conform fully to type. As you would expect, most of the available research material has concentrated on the Northern hemisphere, particularly Europe. If the seasonal-food point is valid, we also need to consider samples from, say, opposite bits of the Northern hemisphere. If climatic conditions are crucial, we need a Southern hemisphere sample.

In general terms, the best you can say is that the correlations so far identified are statistically interesting without being significant for our purposes. However, several people known to the author will go on checking birth dates and retreating to their bookshelves to make comparisons. Do make your own checks, because if only a few job/star links can be proven, they may be just as good as gut feel, instinct, bad interviews and prejudice. They beat palmistry and phrenology, too.

Best by Test

It is no secret that the author has reservations about the merits of interviews as a basis for assessing people, whether they are at the arm's length or already employees. Of all the possible alternatives, formal tests offer the greatest potential for objective assessment.

It may be helpful if we look at possible tests in a fairly pragmatic way. It is not enough just to comment about the excellence of the test under ideal conditions. There are other factors which dictate whether a particular test or tests may be worth including as part of your filtering process:

- how easy are they to administer?
- how long do they take?
- who can score them?
- do they need a qualified interpreter?
- can they be self-administered?
- are they threatening to the victim?
- are the results unequivocal and devoid of jargon?

Several of these may appear expedient rather than just pragmatic. This is unfortunate but true, yet it does not invalidate their use as a basis for using a particular test. There is always a balance to be struck between perfection and practicality. A cheap and cheerful test which can be widely applied without frightening the victims may be more use than the most sophisticated, which takes too long to decipher and may only produce results after the sitter has left the premises. Tests which damage the victims' performance in the subsequent meeting may also be counter-productive.

In consequence, some fairly simple tests are very widely used although better, more thorough, examples exist. Equally, pragmatic assessors retreat to things like graphology, scored bio-data, reference-checking, astrology and sudden-death telephone interviews rather than interview everyone or test them on site. Sticking for the moment to tests *per se,* some guidance on the possible choice may be appropriate.

First, let us think about IQ. As part of our research we talked at length to D. Mackenzie Davey, the doyen of UK occupational psychologists, about his personal preferences in the test field. He sets great store by intelligence tests as the core of a test programme. There is no substitute for intelligence, which shines through almost regardless of education. He made the point that nearly all entrepreneurs are bright, although intelligence alone is not enough. Other tests are needed to indicate how the subject applies intelligence.

You are probably familiar with the range of IQ tests available, although most of us were exposed to Cattell's example, or Wechsler, during our development. Other tests may hint at intelligence levels, assessed by numerical, verbal or spatial standards, but there is no substitute for a conventional IQ test.

Personality comes next. The old favourite is the 16PF, again from George Cattell, covering sixteen personality factors, but broadly used to assess emotional stability. In its crudest form, users will focus on two key areas:

- is the subject introverted or extrovert?
- is he or she stable, neurotic or where in between?

There are lots of other things you can derive from this or its more sophisticated younger cousin, the Savile and Holdsworth OPQ, but both demand translation by a trained practitioner. Even the translations can be dangerous in the hands of someone who does not understand the jargon.

For example, the author once read a narrative translation of a potential colleague's 16PF which said, like the 16PF chart

Tests—are they threatening
to the victim?

itself, that the subject had a very low level of anxiety. To the novice reader this seemed fine. The aim was to run a cheerful happy partnership, devoid of stress and indeed anxiety. Alas, a low anxiety level also implies that the subject doesn't get anxious over things other reasonable people would *rightly* get anxious about, like:

- meeting deadlines
- the effect of their indiscipline on colleagues
- clients going mad with anxiety over their laid-back perception of a joint problem . . .

None of these are good for business.

Another of the author's favourite tests is the Myers Briggs, on management style and, by implication, team behaviour. This is reasonably non-threatening to the subject, in that it is short and victims can be told in advance that what comes out is merely going to place them in one of the sixteen boxes which cover the possible permutations of four characteristics:

> Extroversion v Introversion
> Sensing v Intuitive
> Thinking v Feeling
> Judging v Perceiving

A further advantage of this test is that it is scored numerically and the raw result which marks you as an INTJ (intuitive is an N, by the way, all the others follow their initial letters) rather than an ESFP, for example, comes up from a few minutes' addition and perhaps a re-check when you don't believe the result. It can get more complex if you score in the middle of any pair or you are close to the centre line, but for these nuances the data can be passed to an expert who will interpret the shades of grey.

This test does not make value judgements, it merely suggests likely behavioural style. However, it does permit you to build teams which are complementary rather than a set of clones. This is particularly important if you want to avoid having lots of entrepreneurs and no workers – a classic problem in service businesses.

It also gives great comfort if you want someone to replicate a particular performer to know that he or she comes firmly in the same box as the existing old reliable. However, it does not assess intelligence or neuroses, so it needs to be used in conjunction with other filters if you want a total view of the person.

Because of this team-building potential, it is a very useful tool for assessing the people you already have, so as to make best use of their merits or move them away from things which are alien to their style. It can therefore give you an extra insight before appraisal or counselling meetings.

In particular, you get the chance to balance your entrepreneurs and innovators with 'enablers' and traditional 'bureaucrats' (the last are the largest minority, by the way), which must help. Too many 'entrepreneurs' are a pain in the neck, even in a high-level consultancy business, although it is interesting to note that Japan has more than twice as many 'entrepreneur' types as the UK management sample and less than half the number of 'bureaucrats' . . .

Other little gems emerge which you are not going to pick up in any normal interview. We talked at length with Dr Andrew Stewart of Informed Choice, who pointed out the different behaviour patterns of each type under stress. For instance, they break down, so to speak, as follows:

> type ST becomes dogmatic
> the SF becomes depressive
> an NT (like the author), obsessive
> and NF? hysterical!

Even a stress interview isn't going to give you that sort of information reliably every time.

As with all tests, experiment gently until you are comfortable; trying them out on people you know can help build your understanding of the tests. In a few extreme cases, you can even guess people's types before you test them. This, of course, is frowned upon, but it's still fun.

In the final analysis, what you want is an indication of how people will behave in a normal situation and it is useful to be able to predict that John is likely to behave like Hamilton, and Wendy, you realize with fascination, just like like Patrick. The thrill is waiting to see if George will behave like Mark and Martin; or perhaps, since one or more of them actually scored very close to the centre line on some characteristics, the comparison is invalid. At least the scores are numeric, very accessible and can be rechecked later, to help your understanding of both the test and the individuals.

However, personality types or styles (the author prefers the former word, but the latter is the official designation) are not enough. What can we learn from tests that will tell us whether someone is going to succeed or not? Mackenzie Davey suggests two key causes of failure. The first, as you would deduce from his earlier comments, is that the poor performers are just not bright enough. The second, that they are not robust enough emotionally. This does not necessarily mean that they break down spectacularly but that they may proceed without adequate attention, as if on autopilot. He also made the intriguing comment that extreme work performance may actually be a neurotic symptom which, unless and until it becomes uncontrolled, can lead to spectacular successes!

Again, it is worth mentioning that there are relatively few interviewers whose experience or command of an interview is going to enable them to identify personality extremes which could spill over into performance failures or anomalies in the workplace, whereas a relevant battery of psychometric tests, professionally interpreted, stands a reasonably good chance of highlighting potential problems.

Given the vast number of tests available, it is not possible to list them all here, nor would it be sensible to pick them from a list without professional guidance. It is more important that you choose a psychologist whose understanding of your problems you feel comfortable with and take his or her advice on the mix of tests appropriate to your needs. Nearly all the 'proprietary' tests available have to be scored, interpreted and in most cases administered by a professional, so a thorough pursuit of the testing route starts with the choice of your adviser in this area. As with insurance, be fractionally more cynical about buying a test from the person or firm which invented it. Your tame psychologist is likely to be more impartial (and may be more balanced about its limitations). Useful guidance in this whole area is offered in *Psychological Testing* by John Toplis, Vic Dulewicz and Clive Fletcher (IPM, 1987).

Graphology

Graphology works. It has limitations which make it unsuitable as a sole selection tool but as an aid to pre-selection, in the hands of an expert, it is well worth considering. The reservations are important. It is not to be used by amateurs or the trained but inexperienced. You need to test the graphologist against a known sample of people and beware of Barnum words, yet graphology can permit you to whittle down a mass of written applications, where track records are brief or unavailable (graduates, school-leavers, etc.), provided your criteria are clear to the graphologist. Equally, unusual personality traits may show up in handwriting without being overt at interview. This can permit an interviewer to probe better or make a case for formal testing, unless and until you have total confidence in the graphologist.

In the author's experience, the good graphologist is best at producing a nutshell view of an individual which is less extensive, but sometimes more incisive, than formal personality tests. It is significant that, when we have hired somewhat odd consultants, clearer warnings have come in the graphologist's report than in the various psychometric test translations.

Before making use of this particular aid, the author conducted a fairly objective test on a sample of executives in a client company, comparing the test results against the candidates' appraisal records and the personnel function's views on them. The first test was to see if the personnel people could identify the managers in the sample by reading their anonymous assessments. This was not a problem. There was a 100 per cent correlation between the reports and the victims. Even the author, who had previously worked with some of the sample at Ford, had no difficulty on the ones he knew.

The next step was to go more thoroughly through the reports, eliminating 'Barnum words' which could apply to almost any-one, and see if we could get a better than average match between the reports and past work performance. Again, the match was much better than coincidence could justify. Additionally, the graphologist identified several short-term pressures and weaknesses which were not evident from the previous appraisal records but could be validated by recent feedback from line boss and/or peer group.

In one case, the graphologist's report indicated cardiac problems which had only just been identified by the patient's GP. As a result of this exercise, the graphologist in question has since been recommended to clients, with considerable success. It was logical to use him as a source for comment in this chapter. He is Alan Bishop and he has worked extensively both in selection and internal appraisal. Typically, he is used as a complement to the interview proocess and he does not recommend that even a skilled practitioner should replace it entirely.

However, he suggests three ways in which graphology can be applied in the selection context. First, once the candidate specification is known, the handwriting samples can permit a broad-brush first filter which will eliminate the largely unacceptable personality profiles. Second, for the minority who look tolerable and worthy of interview, the adviser can produce for each candidate a pre-interview analysis which can assist the recruiter to decide on an interview programme and assess which points to probe in depth. Third, for the minority whom the employer wishes to take further, a deeper report can be prepared which will complement the interview results. In recent samples, this 'Impact Analysis' identified personality problems which were not evident at interview but very evident in later work performance. This, you may feel, tells us more about the interviewers than about graphology, but the fact remains that the candidates were facing a battery of professional recruiters whose interview-based judgements had been successful in hundreds of client appointments.

Alan Bishop also stresses the benefits of an additional filter which can be applied without subjecting the candidates to more meetings and more visits over heavier interview programmes or test-based assessment. In particular, he is able, like the psychometric testers we consulted, to quote cases where the poor interviewee had shown up better in his supplementary filter and later performed well in-job, although the interview result would have placed him (or her) second or third.

Phrenology

People who believe in phrenology are few and, for our purposes, should be fewer. It would be ungracious to suggest that they need their heads examined. We mention it only to point out that selection methods based on decisions about any aspect of anatomy and physiognomy are without statistical and research support and can be discounted for our purposes, except as a guide to the intelligence and thought processes of anyone you discover using them as a selection tool. This brings us to a useful additional filter. Just as most criticism tells you something about the critic as well as the subject, the user of a patently fat-headed selection technique is offering you another way of assessing him or her . . .

Palmistry

Sherlock Holmes used to discover things about people from the state of their hands, not just palms, but he was generally making a distinction between the horny-handed sons of toil and the sedentary clerks of this world. The process is not going to be much help to you unless you are trying to assess whether someone after a manual job has been doing it lately, or at all. However, palmistry *per se* is most unlikely to be useful as a selection tool, not least because to use it you need the victim's presence and co-operation. Would you really want them to form an opinion of your organization as one which used tests for which there is no real support from any authoritative source?

Palmistry

Medicals

You might like to consider whether, for many senior and sensitive jobs, a medical examination is as important as the interview. And whether, for some manual jobs, it might not be more important . . .

References

Conventional references are not rated highly in recent studies of assessment methods. Rightly so, if we mean the formal written request to certify that a particular candidate is honest, sober, trustworthy, hard-working and clean about the house. Even the most helpful employer, aware of the statutory caveats against giving adverse references to a past employee which differ from the declared reasons for firing them (or merely aware of the law on defamation), will often give a written reference which is favourable on all these points even though the employee was paranoid, neurotic, offensive, incompetent, stupid, a poor manager, sexually cavalier and unloved.

In order to get over this barrier, you need to use some or all of the following ingredients:

(a) if you do it in writing, send a copy of the job description and ask if the candidate could do that *specific* job well
(b) invite a telephoned reply or indicate that you will phone them
(c) go to past, not present, employers *before* making an offer. The post-offer reference is less helpful and logistically difficult if it goes bad. Worse, you may be tempted to ignore it if you or your colleagues have already committed the company

(d) where possible, go to a referee of your choice, perhaps a part of your professional network, rather than the candidate's nominee

(e) ideally, if it can be done without breaching your actual or implied obligations of confidentiality to the candidates, take up such references discreetly before meeting them. For instance, you can present the request on the basis that you are thinking of making an approach to the candidate, rather than suggesting he or she has applied to you.

Put some or all of these into action and the defective conventional reference can be transformed into a powerful tool. In particular, referees of stature generally take professional pride in demonstrating their impartiality, if approached in the correct context. Although they may not like the individual, there is usually a grudging assessment of the way they would do the job, warts and all.

Scored Biodata

To save time, the author should stress that he is in favour of scored biodata, at both a formal and informal level. The process has several merits, although the formal proprietary application may be too cumbersome for amateur and short-run use. It demands a substantial degree of preparation, by an expert, including the use of a formal structured candidate specification and associated application forms to permit the scoring and weighting to take place in a common form. Even the experts recognize that it is most appropriate to volume recruitment.

However, there is also an informal version which probably does not deserve the formal title but nevertheless involves a review of biodata and some attempt at weighting and scoring. We refer to the long-standing discipline of comparing the candidate's career history, evidenced on CV or application form, with a good candidate specification to determine whether there is an adequate match which would justify proceeding further.

If the application form or a supplementary questionnaire has been properly prepared, there should be enough information available to permit this comparison *before* an interview programme is arranged, so that the interview process only involves people substantially relevant to the candidate requirement.

In a less than perfect situation, the scoring has to be carried out after the interview, which is used to some extent as the completion of the information-gathering exercise.

Some of the merits of the informal system are immediately obvious:

- the creation of a good job specification becomes essential
- the use of a tailored application form or supplementary questionnaire is also indicated, although not absolutely essential
- using the process enforces forethought and structure in a process often performed with little thought and no structure (this is perhaps unfair to the many worthy and competent interviewers who have regarded this as the right and natural way to approach the interview process).

There is a snag. On the one hand, people who adopt the informal system are performing a satisfactory step in the *selection* process. On the other hand, they may be fooling themselves into thinking that they are achieving excellence in *interviewing*, when the interview has merely become the last stage in a process of data collection. All the time which could have been spent refining on this may have been wasted. That they do not realize this may be due to the fact that bad interviews are so bad, and even an informal data-collection and scoring system so much better than the average interview, that this approach can be an effective alternative to the interview proper. Could it be that the majority of successful 'interviews' are run on these lines?

It is important to find out what your colleagues are doing. If they are ignoring the benefits of 'amateur' data scoring, they can with advantage be educated. If they are applying the technique without knowing it, they can be encouraged to do more of it in the pre-interview phase, so leaving the interview time for a better exchange – and reducing the number of interviews. And if they are doing it reasonably well already, they may be a good foundation for your corporate 'better interviewing programme'.

PRELIMINARIES

---

*Inadequate interview
preparation wastes time,
money and the
best candidates*

Communication, Before and After

One major problem in the periods before and after the interview is that you lose candidates because they lose interest. Apart from the need for speed and information which will retain their interest, you can improve the quality of contact with them by using the telephone. Letters, although administratively tidy and useful where matters of record are involved, do not permit total two-way communication. Telephone calls do.

There is therefore an overwhelming case for using the telephone both before and after interview, for several reasons:

- it can permit you to verify whether an interview is really necessary
- it can ensure that you increase the better candidates' interest before interview
- it can help eliminate minor communication failures after interview and create a bond with candidates to whom you may want to make an offer
- equally, if you make contact and a candidate is under pressure from another employer, it permits you to speed up your reaction
- alternatively, a courtesy call during which a marginal candidate tells you of uncertainties can permit you to retain their interest or allow them to self-reject, saving you the trouble, mildly bad PR and embarrassment of turning them down in writing later.

This principle applies in other areas of people relations, and beyond. Letters, where telephone calls could be used, imply an unwillingness to communicate. They also offer delay, partial communication, the scope for misunderstanding that a one-way message always offers and the uncertainty of not knowing whether the message was received. Apart from that, they're fine.

This also means that your offer ought to be communicated orally (either at a meeting or by phone) before it is confirmed in writing, if at all possible, unless there are genuine tactical arguments against.

Documentation

One of the themes running through this book, although not signalled as such, is the need to get some things down in writing, partly so that there can be agreement about them in advance, as with candidate specifications. A good corporate description and job description are an essential part of the communication with candidates – and indeed with existing employees, if one is to counsel and appraise them in the right context. However, the need for adequate structured documentation before and during the interview is less well recognized. Most interviewers take notes. Rather fewer structure them so that they relate specifically to the criteria on which the selection process is allegedly based. Fewer still do so in a format which would enable the interviewer to go back in six months' time and say with any credibility that the notes were valid predictors of the candidate's later performance. This may be because the notes are not good enough, or because the interview was not good enough, or both. However, if we are to achieve improvements in the interview process, several things have to happen:

- such documentation must exist
- it must be in a form which the interviewers and their colleagues can understand later, and
- it must be in a form which permits a qualitative post-audit.

The idea of a post-audit is not popular, but it can be presented as having three distinct benefits:

- the need for the post-audit enforces better documentation
- if the interview is a defective tool, you can only find out how bad it is with retrospective analysis of this kind
- if there are diehards among your colleagues who believe passionately in the interview, it offers them a basis on which to prove their point, so you can all identify what they are doing which is making their interviews better than the national norm.

This last benefit may help sell the concept of post-audit, and the

the good practice leading to it, to otherwise unsympathetic colleagues who are unreasonably proud of the old ways. Finally, good discipline on documentation ensures, for all types of interview, a better chance that the interviewer will note what has to be done next!

One other bonus flows from good documentatioin. When you get to the end of an interview programme and nobody meets the candidate specification, you can choose to lower your criteria retrospectively, but you can only do this methodically if the criteria and the candidates' match thereto are carefully and qualitatively recorded. Quite often this pragmatic rethink may be preferable to a new resourcing campaign, not just because it is cheaper and quicker but because your interview programme has taught you more about what is available and the art of the possible may be appropriate.

Documentation in the run-up to appraisal and counselling interviews is equally important. It is not adequate to rely on word-of-mouth preliminaries, because people mishear or hear what they fear. As with new products, give them a chance to read the instructions. By all means tell them too, but if they don't have a bit of paper which helps remind them what has been said, the later interview will be flawed by misunderstanding or foreboding.

It is also important to have a contemporary note of what was discussed and agreed at the meeting. This need not be formal. One manager we know produces a manuscript note during the discussion which is photocopied at the end of the session so that both parties have a copy. This is pleasantly informal and looks as if the victim has been a party to the creation of the document. Actually, the manager in question is often working from a crib sheet underneath the bit of paper on which he is writing – visible from above but not at an angle – but the beneficial effect is unimpaired and the structure is more assured. Do not expect appraisal and counselling subjects to remember all that has been said. Human nature is not like that and they are under stress. Even promotion can be stressful . . .

Recruitment: Pre-interview Planning

This problem is unique to the recruitment interview. With most other interviews you do not have to worry whether there are going to be enough interviewees. They work for the organization and barring inept administration, will be present and correct when required. In the recruitment process you have to work harder. Not only do you have to tempt them to come to interview, you have to find them before you tempt them.

This is not a book about recruitment as a whole, but it must be stressed that the resourcing decisions have to be sound if the interview programme is to be worthwhile. There are similarities with the purchasing function. You need an adequate supply of candidates in the right place at the right time and, incidentally, at the right price. The right choice of sources ensures this supply. There is also a quality-control aspect. As with purchasing, you wish to ensure that all the candidates are of adequate quality. Given that they are people rather than inanimate objects, this implies that they are also interested in the job, with a clear idea of what the job is.

The first requirement demands that you apply adequate resources, so that you do not miss candidates you would wish to meet and do not meet candidates you would wish to miss. Inadequate resourcing can prevent you being in touch with the former and, because you are desperate, tempt you to meet the latter.

Good processing then ensures that you give the candidates enough data prior to interview for some degree of self-selection to take place. In other words, the people who do not fit the job get a chance to decide this before (and instead of) being interviewed. This process is further enhanced if the resourcing exercise involves adequate disclosure by the candidates so that you can make a thorough pre-interview decision about their relevance. In the section on Scored Biodata you will be reminded of the desirability of having an application form or brief questionnaire tailored to the vacancy so that a better pre-interview judgement can be made.

The ideal, by the way, is to meet only people who are potentially of short-list calibre. People are seldom dramatically better than their paperwork and it is no use interviewing marginal candidates in the vain hope that one or more of them may be hiding their light under a bushel. This is a waste of time. Far better to sharpen up the recruitment advertising or equivalent and attract the right people while repelling the wrong ones!

There are special pitfalls in the interview if you choose a sourcing technique which is not appropriate to the vacancy. For instance, if you headhunt at too junior a level and the interviewer is not aware that the candidate is a headhunt product or does not appreciate the implications, it is possible for both parties to be expecting the other to sell to them. Worse, the candidate expects to be tempted with large sums of money which, in view of the grading structure, are not available at that level. This can prevent communication between two parties who ought to be able to get together, had they not started wrong.

There are other pitfalls in the pre-interview process. If you interview someone who realizes that he or she has wasted the journey and their time because you did your filtering badly, this reflects badly on the organization and may prevent you hiring them in the future for the right job. If you invite them to interview and they do not realize the mismatch, they can be equally offended, with the same results, when you later reject them.

There is another reason why it is wrong to have too many applicants replying to an advertisement. Unless, and this is very rare, there is a genuine glut of people meeting your criteria, an excess of applicants means that the advertisement was not specific enough. It is no good defending such imprecision by pretending it gives you a better choice. It does not. If your criteria are not clear in the advertisement, there are two horrid possibilities. The first is that they are not clear in the job specification, so your choice is blurred anyway. The second is that the criteria are known but have not been declared, so the respondents are deprived of the chance to demonstrate that they can meet them. They cannot be expected to guess at factors omitted from the advertisement, so the process of filtering the paperwork becomes a lottery. This can be partially corrected by sending candidates a good brief with a full specification of the requirements, but you have still missed candidates who would have applied if they had appreciated their relevance.

All this assumes that you got the resourcing right. As hinted earlier, poor resourcing decisions magnify the problems of interview planning. Typically, in searching for a cost-effective source, it is possible to use sources which are slow, costly and ineffective, although not all at the same time.

Given that you have a choice of using direct advertising, in national or specialist media, agencies, PER, Job Centres, consultants, headhunters, staff introductions, a trawl of the outplacement market or even a review of write-in candidates and people who have left you in the past, any error in assessing the appeal of a job can tempt you to use these sources one by one rather than in parallel. This ensures that at no time do you have enough candidates to constitute a valid shortlist, so there is a continual temptation to wait for the products of the next source before making a decision. By the time you have worked through a big enough sample and realized that the first person you interviewed was the art of the possible, he or she has got fed up with waiting and either decided to accept another offer or decided to reject yours when you make it because you are patently so indecisive. Worse, you have wasted a lot of time. Worse still, you have probably wasted a lot of money.

It may even be that because the interviewing programme has been damaged by the delay, you have seen one or more candidates who would have been acceptable; because memory and documentation are inadequate, they were not correctly identified as potentially employable in the early stages. This is doubly possible if the candidate specification was unclear or non-existent.

This is still about planning, or the lack of it. The solution is a correct estimate of the difficulty of filling a particular job. Any underestimate invariably pitches you down the slippery slope of delay, frustration and a sometimes desperate appointment of the wrong candidate. Other things being equal, if the job is worth doing, it is better to apply a degree of overkill rather than to under-resource. The hidden costs and nuisance implicit in an extended recruitment programme do not show up as clearly as direct recruitment costs, but they exist and can be massive.

'I'm so sorry no one told you we're headhunters, Mr Mablewhite.'

Preparation

Without wishing to encourage semantic disputes, preparing for an interview is not the same as the planning beforehand. Preparation, in this context, implies the detailed work immediately prior to a specific meeting, as against planning, on a wider scale, for the programme as a whole. This preparation includes the provision of a suitable environment, devoid of gratuitous stress and interruption, together with adequate supporting paperwork and other aids.

It also involves, for all types of interview, a peaceful review of the relevant papers. Whether we are considering appraisal, recruitment, counselling or warnings and dismissals, only a paragon can do a decent job off the cuff, reading the paperwork as the interview proceeds, not least because (in recruitment) there should have been some attempt to compare the candidate's records with the specification criteria.

Every type of interview is vulnerable to the omissions and misdirection implicit in poor preparation. There is a further problem if the interviewer has patently not done the necessary homework, in that the interviewee's respect and attention are forfeit; even if the rest of the performance is sound and correct conclusions are reached, they may be discredited in the victim's eyes. As a result, candidates may reject a job offer which would have been right for them and the company, employees appraised may feel somehow cheated of their rights, those counselled will attach less weight to the counsel, or those warned will understand the message imperfectly because they have been distracted by the evident incompetence of the procedure (which may even be such as to invalidate the warning, if a gross error is made).

Preparation, therefore, involves knowing why the victim is there, ensuring that he or she is also aware, warning them if the event is going to take an unusually long time because of supplementary interviews, tests, etc., knowing whether the process is one of recruitment or selection (are you hiring everyone suitable you see or making a choice?) and the means by which the candidate has been induced to come. This last is rather important. A headhunted candidate has been seduced into coming by a process very different from the respondent to an advertisement. Insensitive treatment can waste the cost of the headhunt and make you and the organization look incompetent.

Similarly, the quality of pre-briefing may vary dramatically as between one agency and another. Some agencies brief better than some consultancies. Others may have persuaded a candidate to come along (who therefore arrives without a serious interest in the job) because they know that your organization is particularly good at winning over rare cold specimens. If the interviewer is not aware of this hidden agenda, the meeting might as well not take place.

It can also be necessary to see a copy of the advertisement which lured the victim in. There are very few cases where the advertisement is an exact paraphrase of the full job description, and the candidate criteria may also have been truncated. If a candidate knows he or she fits the requirements in the advertisement perfectly and the interviewer is aware of a shortfall as against the requirements in the full specification, the candidate may be deprived of the chance to make a case for the relevance of his or her background. This is particularly disastrous if a candidate fully meets all the criteria but, because the ad copy was inadequate, has not mentioned the missing skills or experience on the CV or application form.

This problem is eliminated if you use a 'customized' application-form supplement for the particular job. Nothing special – just a single page of A4 paper which asks candidates to indicate how well they fit the specification. This simple communication aid is sadly under-utilized but would save thousands of hours of interview time, either by avoiding the necessity for interviewing people who cannot meet the specification but tend to be interviewed in desperation, on the off chance that they have hidden merits not fully brought out in their CV, or by focusing attention on the relevant minority.

It also aids self-selection. Candidates, confronted with selection criteria which they do not meet, are given a chance either to withdraw before interview or to make a case for taking a risk on their slim experience. Without adequate early disclosure, these options are not available.

The tailored application or issue of a full job description and specification, therefore, encourage better practice and enhance your image to candidates, who may also be customers. Indeed, there is a case for treating all candidates as potential customers. Even slobs buy high-value products and services.

Running Order

Most experienced interviewers have firm views about the merits of telling candidates about the organization and the job before they tell you about themselves – or vice versa. This is not the sort of book which catalogues the arguments on the one hand and on the other with scrupulous fairness. There isn't the space. However, the arguments in favour of putting candidates in the picture first are compelling (with one exception which we shall cover later):

- most candidates can exercise a degree of self-selection; if a job is patently wrong for them will say so, particularly if you take the trouble to ask them
- unless they are very stupid, most candidates present themselves better and more fully if they know the context in which they are presenting themselves
- as some of your colleagues are immune to advice, it is likely that the advice given elsewhere in this text about sending out adequate data before a meeting will have been ignored; it is therefore important to start with some hint of the context
- it provides a warming-up period during which the candidate can get used to the event and limber up with a few tentative questions.

The one exception is for novice interviews, particularly with graduates, where no specific job is in view and one may not be identified until the candidate's interests and merits are disclosed, if then. Even here it may be right to spend a few minutes talking about the company, as a courtesy.

The self-selection process has one snag. Even the most well-balanced candidates may feel cheated if you accept too readily their view that there is not an adequate match between them and the job described. The less fair may even have trouble telling you. It is therefore necessary to find a form of words with which you are comfortable to provoke their opinion, while perhaps also hinting at the possibility of alternative jobs now or in the future. This permits a token review of their merits to close the meeting, so that they can feel they have left some positive impression behind.

> *Three separate hours, unplanned, with three different interviewers will merely yield the same interview thrice*

> *Interviewing, whether you like it or not, is part of your corporate PR effort. Badly planned interviews equal bad PR*

'It's Carruthers' idea to terminate unproductive interviews quickly.'

Interview Overview

At this point, the author is embarrassed. Competent interviewers can skip this bit because it is very basic. On the other hand, even competent interviewers tend to forget at times. The full value of an interview, particularly in recruitment, may be lost if certain minimum criteria are not met. They can be summarized as follows:

- both parties should know why they are there, in advance
- both should have adequate data in writing, in advance if possible
- the environment should be quiet and sympathetic
- there should be no interruptions
- the meeting should start on time
- the furniture should not put the interviewee at a disadvantage, nor the lighting
- both parties should be sure who the other is and any changes in personnel on the employer's part explained clearly
- the interviewer should have done enough homework to know in advance what matters require special attention and to avoid ignorance about matters already covered in the victim's paperwork (this is even more important at counselling and appraisal interviews, where the victim has an extra right to expect the organization to know basic background already)
- the interviewer should plan not to talk much
- the interviewer must control the interview, both as to timing and content, without dominating it
- the interviewer must be prepared to restate what the meeting is to achieve and, at the end, specify what will happen next
- the interviewer must know enough about body language to control his or her own negative reactions!
- the interviewer must know enough about the law to avoid breaches thereof
- the interviewer must know what gaps exist in the basic data about the candidate, as if for scored biodata.

Get all these right and you have a fair chance of running an above-average interview. Omit some and you shoot yourself in the foot before you start.

INTERVIEW CONTENT

In interviews, as elsewhere,
the value of the answer
depends on the quality of
the question

The Loaded Question

The next sections are about the use of questions in interviews. Most of the lessons apply equally to all other management exchanges. The question is the most powerful communication tool in the civilized world, when correctly used. When it is wrongly used or underemployed, communication is reduced or vanishes. Most managers need this tool. Few recognize its importance. In consequence, few plan their use of questions in any meeting. It follows naturally that fewer still plan to train their subordinates in this art.

A few moments' thought about managers you know should bring to mind several who much prefer to make assumptions, rather than suffer the brain strain necessary to think up questions which will elicit facts. 'Don't confuse me with facts, my mind is made up' is used as a joke, but it is also a serious description of these people. The author has sat in meetings with people who, prejudiced by their knowledge of the individual they were discussing, were prepared to fire him for reasons which fitted their stereotype, in spite of the existence of direct and circumstantial evidence which was quite contrary to their assumptions.

An open mind, or at least an ability to remember which of the things in your memory are facts rather than assumptions, plus a battery of relevant questions, must be the best route to management decision-making. Most management activities can be improved thus. Appraisal, buying, counselling, diagnosis, education, problem analysis, recruitment, systems analysis, even selling, can be enhanced. There is a motto outside the management field which runs 'Listen, watch, be silent.' If we added 'except when you are asking sensible questions' the formula would be complete for managerial purposes. It works particularly well in sales, but all of the above activities can be improved by better question design. Not just the avoidance of Yes/No questions; that is not enough. You need to know when to use questions, when a leading question is necessary and what better alternatives are available.

The objective must be to generate, in the right context, answers which are correct, constructive, cohesive and complete. The truth, the relevant bits of the truth and nothing but the truth? Avoid the whole truth: that way boredom or madness lies. The benefits to be derived from improved practice are massive:

- better understanding of staff-development needs
- cheaper purchasing of more relevant product
- better staff morale and motivation
- better health
- faster and more effective learning
- successful problem solving
- better, quicker, hiring
- simpler, more relevant DP systems
- more sales, at better margins, on better terms.

One technique which is crucial to the process of improvement is, as already hinted, to strip out all the redundant questions, by a ruthless examination of their worth and relevance. This is not easy, because as children and adults we have all been conditioned by the parental interrogation pattern which typically runs something like:

> 'Johnny, is this yours?'
> 'What is it doing here?'
> 'Why is it soaking wet?'
> 'Are you going to put it in the wash basket?'

Only the final question really matters in terms of getting a practical result out of the exchange. So it is in business, except that you need enough interrogation to verify the facts, on the assumption that the conversation is taking place between two adults behaving as adults – not always a safe assumption, as there may be a tendency for the culprit to role-play a child. If so, you may have to stick to the unhappy structure above in which:

- the first question establishes the context
- the second may be rhetorical
- the third is designed to establish moral ascendancy
- the fourth comes to the point.

Most of these sighting shots should be unnecessary in an adult conversation, but the working population contains all levels of intelligence and behaviour and you have to recognize that a question which obviously leads into an unpleasant subject may be counter-productive. The sighting shot, if in the form of a question to which both sides think they know the answer, may precipitate an evasion which does not help communication and may inhibit the victim's ability to give a straight answer to the next, better, question. All of us have listened to exchanges like this in which the first brutally offensive and aggressive enquiry, because it is so gross, forces a negative reply which destroys any chance of communication thereafter. The white lie stands in the way of any real dialogue.

'Were you fired by Hard Co.?' is the sort of blunt question favoured by aggressive interviewers. Sometimes it elicits an honest response. Often, because it is too blunt, it generates a euphemism which colours any subsequent explanation. Worse, it is a leading question.

Asking 'Why did you leave?' may be better; depending on your view of the answer, more pressure can then be applied by a question which expresses puzzlement at the tactical wisdom of the departure, no matter which side initiated it. Keep chatting about this and the truth will slowly emerge.

For instance, candidates may say they were fired but present it as part of a larger programme. Probe for the numbers involved. If seventy left, with a formal outplacement programme, it looks more credible than if two left, without help or compensation. It is, of course, wholly unfair to make absolute judgements on the basis of this sort of comparison, but you can add it to the store of knowledge you are building up and take a broader view. You can talk about the merits of the dismissal, explore whether it was referred to a tribunal, whether compensation was offered, or sought, whether favourable references are likely to be available and, if unfavourable, what they will say. Ask if formal warnings were previously given. Ask if the candidate understood the reasons for the firm's action. Ask whether, with hindsight, it could have been avoided.

Keep probing, sympathetically, because this is one key area where the golden rule of non-disclosure applies:

Candidates will seldom lie, but they won't volunteer unpleasant truths unless and until you ask

The interviewer is in control and has to ask. Remember Dr Lake's findings – the average interviewer is too nice: disclosure demands that you be firm.

Good questions do not have to be long. Sometimes you may only need what Bernard Ungerson once described as the psychiatrist's grunt. One step on from this you can practise, and encourage in others, Kipling's six honest serving men: How, What, When, Where, Who and Why.

Next come the tiny encouraging phrases which can be delivered almost as the other party takes breath:

> for example?
> for instance?
> tell me more
> can you enlarge on that?

If the statement you have just heard is unclear, but you do not wish to say that you did not understand, either for fear of seeming stupid or of insulting the interviewee, similarly brief phrases need to be constructed:

> in what sense?
> how so?
> elucidate, please
> how would you explain that to a layman? (if the answer was grossly jargon-ridden)

All this is helping the interviewee stretch beyond the stock answer into areas where extra merits, if any, come into the open. One key point in this pursuit is to avoid the accidental leading question. It is terribly easy to ask whether people have done something or if they have experience of X and Y. Avoid the 'whether' and the 'if'. Although they sound normal and conversational, they also lead straight into Yes/No responses. Instead, discipline yourself (and those you delegate to) about the need for asking the supplementary qualitative question *first*. You will be able to construct your own samples, but in the examples above try:

'What have you done in this area?'
'How extensive is your experience of X?'
'Where was your best exposure to Y?'

There are many good reasons for avoiding leading questions, but the danger here is not that the victims will say 'Yes' to the bad question – at least a Yes enables you to ask the right supplementary. Instead, you need to help them not to say 'No', just because they have not been forced to think beyond the easy negative. Although in principle the interviewees are trying to put their best foot foward, the strain of doing so may affect the way their memories work. How often have you left a meeting of any sort and remembered some vital fact or argument which should have been uppermost in your mind? It is a classic problem of the human mind at any time and gets worse under stress. Interviews, even well-conducted ones, constitute stressful situations.

Remember also the tendency for people to be reactive rather than proactive. The line of least resistance is to follow the interviewer's questions unless the victim has come with a personal agenda which can be integrated into the exchange (equally likely in appraisal and recruitment). Since this requires effort, many interviewees take the easy way out in spite of their prepared input.

If you are going to get the best out of any meeting where this inhibition applies, therefore, you have to provide the questions which will make them react, or a catalyst which will make them proactive for a change. This may not be a question. It could be a deliberate attempt to throw the ball back at them and leave them holding it, as in the formula mentioned elsewhere: 'Modesty and space must have prevented you giving a full picture in your CV. Please outline the things you had to leave out which you feel might be relevant to our needs.'

Note that this request avoids any suggestion of duplicating the career biography already on record and demands complementary data. In other words, it forces people to think, probably more widely than any one tight question might have done. Because it is not limited in its range, it may also give the poor old interviewer a breathing space if the interviewee responds constructively and fully. Breathing space for the interviewer is important. You need time to think and plan, although not at the expense of your listening effort!

Listening properly is the only way you are going to generate proper supplementary questions on the points of weakness or high interest. The supplementary questions are always important, because they flow from new material volunteered by the candidate. Even an inadequate answer constitutes new material, because it suggests an area of weakness which, if it is in an 'essential' part of the candidate specification, must be probed.

Additionally, when the questioning indicates something is missing, whether in their technical experience or their achievements against present or recent objectives, ask what they are doing about it. Always ask what the individual is doing about it when he or she laments the absence of anything. There is no one right answer, but you'll get a much better idea of the way people tackle known difficulties if you have have a sample of their reactions to them – or their lack of reaction. If the answer is that they have not done anything, whether or not they tell you why, supplementary questions should always ask what they have thought about doing to correct the omission. This applies both to profit problems and personal weaknesses.

Incidentally, if a 'personality clash' is indicated, they will be aware, as you are, that personality clashes occur between two or more people. It is legitimate and necessary to ask, not whether they were at fault, but whether their style may have contributed to the situation. This turns the subject into a 'no-fault' accident and improves the chances you will get a measured answer.

Again, whatever the answer, probe further. For example, although the ex or present boss may be the worst manager in the Western World, it is important that you know how the individual adapts to such a problem and will cope in future. Ask what they have learned from the situation. Ask how they have coped and will cope in future. Depending on your view of the individual's thought processes, you may find it helpful to ask in reverse chronological order – in other words, ask first what they would do if the circumstances arose again in the future and then go back and ask what they actually did. There will usually be a difference. Exploring this difference will tell you more about the past situation and the personal style – and indeed resilience – of the interviewee.

It may also be a useful point to ask what sort of management style they like practised around them. This can lead naturally into one or more supplementaries. The order will depend on your on-the-spot concern about the credibility of the answers to date, but it is always worth trying to find out:

- what sort of style they want beneath them
- what works best in their peer group
- what they like to report to
- how they train their team to achieve a satisfactory style.

You could also ask what their Myers-Briggs style is. If they have been through a Myers-Briggs test and properly debriefed, they are likely to remember. And it can give you an instant insight into their team behaviour which will help your questioning.

As a further indication of the way they behave in the total team, you could enquire whom they have learned from lately – and what they have learned. There may be some environments in which it is not possible to learn, but anyone who can look back over a whole year and feel that they have learned nothing is likely to have a fairly closed mind. In pursuing this point, you could also ask if their organization has spent time and money on training them recently. Apart from the fact that this is a useful guide to the way the organization perceives them, it may also help remind them that they have actually learned something. And if not, why not?

If you are going back over previous jobs and they appear to be repetitive, give the interviewee a choice. Ask whether there was much to learn or whether it was mostly the application of their past experience. If there appear to be several negative indicators, such as criticism of past bosses or companies, circle round again and test further about the ways they interacted with the past teams. You could try one or more of the following:

- have you developed any special techniques for managing people?
- how do you plan your criticism of subordinates? (then ask them to describe the most recent example)
- what have you been criticized for in the last year? (then ask whether the criticism was valid)

- have you been formally appraised lately? With what results? What action have you taken as a result? Did you learn anything about appraisal systems? Or about yourself? Has it improved the way you run appraisal interviews?
- are you aware of weaknesses that did not show up in appraisals? What have you done about them?

Even if you knit the supplementaries together well, you may find that some interviewees stonewall in this sort of exchange. Back off from the direct attack and come in again asking for examples of recent people-handling problems above, below and around them. It is essential that you cover at least two of these three levels. You could also ask, to refine your view of their views: What irritates you? or What makes you less effective?

Finally, although the question can come up earlier in the conversation, always ask whether they have identified a successor and whether the successor is ready to take over. Do *not* ask if they have trained a successor – the answer will always be in the affirmative. Instead, see if their earlier answers suggest that they may have done so. If they have given no hint, ask how they are preparing the successor. The word 'preparing' encourages them to consider a wide answer if the reality is wider than training and it does not force them into a white lie about training if the preparation process has been something other (and perhaps less) than a training plan.

The same technique applies to other areas of questioning. A broad enquiry avoids leading the witness into the specifics implied by some narrow verbs. This principle applies too in the supportive questioning which forms part of appraisal and counselling interviews. Even nice questions like 'Can we help?' invite a Yes/No answer; if the answer is No, you have an extra problem trying to probe further, whereas if you had said '*How* can we help?' the chances of a constructive dialogue are improved.

All this is not easy. It involves a careful review of your speech patterns, to eliminate forms and phrases you may have used for many years. Do persevere.

There is a bonus. If you clean up your act in this way, the quality of communication in your domestic and other social life may improve too. If you do not regard this as a good thing, that is another problem, but the cleaning-up process is important at work not just because it will improve interviews but because it offers the chance to improve all interactions. Discipline on this front can improve your performance as a manager and make you respected as the only person around who gets results, understands, cares, thinks straight or talks sense. Any and all of these can flow from better quality questions at work.

Most people, most of the time, are reactive, so they react to what is evident and miss what is not. Without discipline, this mars every aspect of recruitment, but particularly the interview

The Questions – Exclusions

Emphasis on time constraints suggests an area for improvement: you can make more time by omitting things. In particular, as well as planning the questions you propose to ask, there are continual opportunities to eliminate unplanned questions – or even the planned but obsolete kind. These must include:

- the irrelevant
- those asked only to fill silences
- the illegal
- other discriminatory questions
- the trivial (do you really need to waste much time on hobbies, sport, family – beware the discriminatory! – school, ancestors, siblings or dogs . . .?)
- politics.

In this general area, a minefield for the bad interviewer and at best a quicksand for the average, the opportunity to open your mouth and put your foot in it has always been great, but with current legislation there are real and compelling penalties for error. Somewhere in your organization there will be one or more old-style interviewers who in a few minutes of unguarded paternal chat can lay the foundation of a massive case of discrimination just by asking comfortable (well, he's comfortable with them) questions which identify not one but several grounds on which the organization might appear to be discriminating. One white middle-aged interviewer being 'supportive' to a black female single parent whom he has decided to reject on non-discriminatory grounds can ask enough questions to get an industrial tribunal writhing in embarrassment later, almost without him drawing breath, just because he wants to stretch out the interview to a reasonable length.

These people are time-bombs. As indicated elsewhere, some don't know the law. Others know it but believe they are exempt – perhaps by custom and practice? Find them. Educate them. Or stop them interviewing!

Favourite Questions

In preparation for this book, the author invited his contacts to contribute their favourite interview questions. The sample below is presented without comment, except that some of the worst have been included as well as the best . . .

'There is no job description – when you join, will you help us write one?'

'What do you do best in your current job?'

'Do you like Borneo?'

'What is the best measure of performance in a job like that?'

'How did you go about the task of managing others?' (followed by 'Yes, but what exactly did you do to motivate them?')

'What evidence is there of . . .?' (i.e. what solid achievements are available as a result of your efforts?)

'How would you expect your results to be judged if you were appointed to this position?'

'What is the most difficult decision you have ever had to make – and why?'

'Tell me about depreciation' (in whichever foreign lanaguage the candidate professes to speak best, followed, for his or her second-best language, by a social question rather than a technical one).

'As this is the only interview, do you have any questions, no matter how silly they may seem, about the Company, department, position or me, which you might wish you had asked if we offer you that job?'

'What do you plan to do if you don't get this position?'

'Are you user-friendly?'

'When you quit, what will your boss say?'

'What changes in your present environment would stop you applying for other jobs?'

'This CV looks like a general handout. If you were writing it in the context of this particular job, what changes would you make'?

And, finally, a stinker which was used on one contributor: 'What would you do if you saw a battleship in a wood?' The correct answer, according to Nick Cowan, is 'Change my liquor.' We are also indebted to Berry Wilson, Stephen McNeile, Penelope Cammiade, D.E. Ridgley, Hugh McCredie, Bob Ponting, Colin Harrison and Alastair Mowat for the other quotes.

Sneaky Questions

Although, as indicated earlier, we are not in favour of stress interviews or exam-type questions out of context, there is a case for making your questions demanding. The Lake study mentioned in the Introduction pointed out that UK managers tend to be too nice about their interview conduct.

This should not extend to the quality of the questions. Being bland and anodyne may be very soothing for the candidates, but it is unlikely to increase their respect for you or your organization – or for the job offer if one emerges.

Instead, do consider asking questions which tax the candidates' memory and intelligence. For example, a two-part or three-part question will indicate their ability to recall and deal with these in a work situation. Nothing is more depressing than a colleague who forgets the second item on a list because of the mental strain involved in dealing with the first. You are entitled to be deeply suspicious of their ability to cope with even the simplest multiple instructions in the workplace.

Similarly, for more senior candidates a question which implies a simple algorithm is helpful in determining intellectual application. Here again you can probe for an ability to distinguish between facts and assumptions. This is best done in supplementary questioning, probably after the candidate has delivered a sweeping judgement about past or present employers or colleagues; you can then legitimately ask what factors led them to those conclusions. If the answer is less than convincing, ask in a different way what objective evidence they have to support the conclusion. If they prevaricate, probe again round the edges. Ask, perhaps, if there is also circumstantial corroboration? If you are still unconvinced (some people don't understand what circumstantial evidence is), ask whether the victims of the criticism would agree with it. If the answer is positive, ask why. If negative, ask what other factors the victims might adduce in their favour.

Keep on probing until you either agree with the likely truth of the criticism or the culprit recognizes that the criticism might have been too sweeping and is reasonable enough to say so. Alternatively, you may be forced to the conclusion that they are incapable of recognizing the nature of your concern and their suitability for working close to you is at once in doubt.

Don't be afraid to make the candidates think. Their ability to do so may be crucial to the way your business runs after they join you; if you don't find out beforehand, you do them and your existing team a grave disservice.

'Any questions?'

The Ubiquitous Question

It is possible and desirable to structure your own interview questions so that they provoke questions from the candidate. As indicated elsewhere, this can be done by asking deliberately obscure questions, but the principle can also be extended. This is because their questions are likely to be a better guide to their interests, motivation, personality and thought processes than conventional answers to your conventional questions.

For example, if you ask: 'What interests you most about us and the job? you are likely to get a pre-packaged reply, probably true but not deep. Alternatively, if you ask 'What more do you want to know about us and the job?' and keep asking it in different ways through a chain of supplementary questions, you will almost certainly get a wider view which focuses on matters of most interest or concern, including:

- rewards
- security
- prospects
- opportunities to contribute
- power
- problems sought
- other insecurities
- style, and sometimes
- prejudices.

There is an old saying: 'If you don't ask, you won't get.' We can amend this: 'If you don't ask, they may not ask either.'

That Uncertain Question

Much of this book is about being precise and understandable. However, there is also a case for sometimes being *imprecise* under controlled conditions, because by doing so you may force a reaction from the candidates. That reaction (or lack of it) will tell you more about them.

Specifically, plan to use words or phrases which have two (or more) meanings. This will have one of three results, two of them acceptable. The first is that the candidate will answer the question on both levels, the second that he or she will ask for clarification, and the third that he/she assumes one meaning and answers only that option.

Unless the question is very complex, the first choice may be the right one. If the answer has to be cumbersome, you may have learned that the candidate in question is intelligent and tactful, but not too assertive. The second is usually the preferable pattern, because the candidate has demonstrated both awareness and assertion, which in a work situation (and this is in some ways a work sample) could be crucial. The third is worrying. Perhaps the candidate was not listening. Perhaps not bright enough to identify the problem. Perhaps not assertive enough to take issue with the interviewer or appear to criticize.

Let us take a specific example. If you ask 'what systems improvements have you initiated?' to anyone who is not in computing, it could imply any of the following:

- computer systems
- accounting systems (or any other manual system of paper processing)
- physical systems in a manufacturing or warehousing and distribution context
- communications systems, or possibly
- another system of handling people.

In most cases, the candidates who want to do a two-level answer can confine themselves to a computer and a particular non-computer context, but most managers in real life will have more than two options if they think carefully about it; they therefore have to ask what is meant or risk a superficial assumption. Do you want to hire people who make assumptions without a clear idea of the facts? Incidentally, this particular question can always be asked, at most staff levels, because all organizations have systems of some kind and most candidates need to be aware of them.

Similarly, at technical and all managerial interviews, it is legitimate to ask what effect the candidate's work has had on their organization's Annual Report. Again, this is deliberately unclear, but what you are probing for is an indication they know what an Annual Report to shareholders actually *is* (that it demonstrates how the organization has fulfilled its corporate objectives in financial terms) and that the effect of any manager's work will have some effect on Profit and Loss Account or Balance Sheet, or both. Any manager who can say that his or her work has had absolutely no effect is also implying that he or she cannot understand how the work contributes or does understand but has not contributed. You could ask which of these is true.

Candidates do have a route out of this trap. If they work in a huge organization and do not have profit-centre or even cost-centre responsibility, they could legitimately claim that their achievements are too small to make much of an impact on the vast numbers involved. This in turn demands a supplementary question from the interviewer: 'If the impact is so small, why does your department exist?'

Keep probing in this area and do not be afraid to keep coming back to accounting matters and financial objectives because, even in a non-profit-making organization, managers are expected to run their departments efficiently and to control costs. In a commercial business, the understanding of the profit motive should be in every manager's mind; if you encounter one who has not realized how his or her local objectives connect up in the grand scale of things, you have identified a potential problem. Even the sales staff who boast about exceeding revenue targets but do not automatically indicate the profit effect may be dangerous. Everything in a business can be justified in financial terms. Even sensitive decisions about safety and welfare are not made solely on humanitarian grounds. Good practice and best practice are not good reasons. Their effect on the survival of the business may be.

There are many other ways you can create deliberately unclear questions, but do be sure that you plan them and are aware of the options. Otherwise you may be doing the candidates and yourself a disservice.

Who's Interviewing Whom?

There is another compelling reason for quality control in the development of your interview questions. Apart from the fact that every time you fail to ask a worthwhile question you waste some of the time in which you could have asked a good one, you may recall the principle that candidates should be judged by the quality of their questions to an equal or greater extent than the quality of their answers. It follows that the good candidates in particular will be judging you and the organization by the quality of your questions.

This is another argument for:

- avoiding all trivial and unplanned questions
- careful construction of the ones you do use
- structuring the interview so that the questions flow logically rather than at random.

The point about unplanned questions applies especially to the amateur interviewer, who tends to ask questions just to fill spaces in the conversation and perhaps give time to the paperwork which he or she is reading, too late, during the meeting. This habit also has the hidden penalty of filling a gap in which the candidate might have said something – or asked something. Friendly pauses are needed, in all types of interview, but particularly with candidates and people being counselled. There is a difference between being in control of an interview, which is necessary and good, and dominating it, which is generally unnecessary and extremely not good.

Additionally, every time interviewers depart from the planned structure without a good reason (supplementary questions flowing from the planned questions are permissible) the context in which a candidate's reactions and behaviour are being assessed starts to differ from that for all the other candidates. If the interviewer says something so fatuous that the candidate spends several seconds not believing it, several minutes being offended by it and the rest of the interview waiting for the next gem to be delivered, his or her performance is going to be affected. It is virtually certain the effect will be adverse.

Worse, the best candidates are likely to be the most perceptive and thus the ones most likely to notice!

Such blunders can also create the sort of appraisal interview which motivates the employee to go out and start reading job advertisements. The reverse can also be true. If an appraisal interview is thorough and successful, it may identify potential which, with or even without training or a development move, can permit you to take a risk on the existing employee and avoid recruitment interviews!

However, do not let this potential bonus blind you to the potential for damage. Any appraisal interview which is less than good is likely to be bad. It is better not to have appraisals than to have a tool for demotivating employees en masse. Many managers, subconsciously recognising this, put off appraisal interviews to the point where the delay is itself a demotivator. You cannot expect any employee who has an overdue appraisal impending to perform normally and, because most variances tend to be adverse, the effect is more likely to be damaging than beneficial. The author can recall one case in which the appraisal interview (and salary review) had been deferred for several months and the manager responsible defended the inaction on the salary front by pointing out that the employee hadn't been performing well . . . for several months!

There is a useful physical law that 'To every action there is an equal and opposite reaction.' Regard it also as a managerial law. *People* are reactive. Even if their managers don't spot the reaction, everything generates some sort of reaction; the grosser the act of omission, the grosser the reaction. Those of you who have encountered the Kepner-Tregoe courses on problem analysis will be familiar with this, in particular the rule for trouble-shooting: to identify the cause of a problem, you go back to the time the problem started and look for *any* change or deviation from the norm around the trouble spot – or even vaguely connected with it.

Every work problem is susceptible to this sort of analysis and, unless the root cause is domestic, the catalyst has probably been some act or omission within the organization. This is not to say that all failures are management failures, but far too many are. It may seem far-fetched to blame personnel problems on badly planned interviews, but they can be part of a larger pattern and an important catalyst – or the last straw.

Proprietary Interviews

Most of this book is about doing things quicker, smarter and otherwise better in-house, in spite of all the (well-founded) reservations about the defects of the traditional unstructured interview. However, there are also proprietary sources of advice and assistance for volume or very sensitive interview pro- grammes. As with scored biodata, an amateur informal version can be attempted on a DIY basis, but to take full advantage of each process (unless you have massive corporate resources and do not mind re-inventing the wheel) you might as well deal with the proprietary sources and decide in discussion with them if their 'products' fit your special needs.

These products are likely to be developed more formally than existing interview examples but may in practice be less threaten- ing and no less informal than a good traditional meeting – and probably more reassuring than a bad one. Where they are likely to differ is in their theme. There are at least two areas where a concentration on specifics must produce more useful results.

One is that the interview concentrates on a work-related core, derived from thorough research among existing job holders, paying particular attention to the profiles of the high and low performers for positive and negative indicators respectively. The resultant criteria and questions are likely to identify candidates' competence in circumstances having a direct connec- tion with the known job and with people showing excellence therein. The emphasis is likely to be on skills and reactions to relevant situations.

The other aspect – probably most important for front-line jobs where candidates are going to be meeting the public without constant (or any) supervision – is the the interview concentrates on attitudes and behavioural traits to determine that candidates have the right personality characteristics to perform well and remain motivated in somewhat lonely positions.

Both these approaches are worthwhile and may indeed overlap or be combined. They have already been shown to have a much better success rate than traditional techniques. Do consider.

Afterthoughts

At the end of an interview, it is not uncommon for the interviewer to find that some vital bit of data has been missed, perhaps because it did not seem important or audible, perhaps because it was not politic to interrupt the candidate's conversational flow. It can therefore be useful to devise a tactful form of words which does not betray your inattention or incompetence.

The author has several, but his favourite is: 'I know you touched on so and so, but I didn't note it fully. Can you tell me about . . .?' This form of words has the added advantage that it remains true even if the reference was a passing one and you didn't really miss anything on the first pass . . .

Remember to use it at the end. Used too soon after the alleged mention it casts severe doubt on your powers of concentration. Used half an hour later it feels human.

RESULTS AND HOW TO GET THEM

Clone recruitment, i.e. recruiting in one's own image, is doubly bad because if two people in an organization always agree, one of them is redundant

Analysis and Action

After any interview, it is important to complete the notes you should have started during it. This is particularly true in recruitment. It is relatively unlikely you will forget the identity of existing employees, although you may well forget what you have asked or offered in counselling and appraisal interviews, but a week later it is possible to be unable to distinguish between the short fat man from Beckenham and the middling chap from Streatham. Sometimes they merge. Sometimes neither of them comes clearly to mind at all.

This makes a compelling case for the rest of your notes being adequate. It also reinforces the earlier point about having clear enough criteria in the candidate specification to know whether, as far as it is possible to determine at interview, the candidate meets them all. How well could they do the job? This must be the key question. If your colleagues can only answer that the individual is not 'our type', the interview process has probably been wasted.

The author has been present at several discussions when the very first candidate was being considered some weeks later as the acceptable minimum, although dismissed at the time as below par. The difficulty at that stage is that nobody has got quite enough data on record to be sure. Equally, when you fill the primary job and the deputy walks out in a huff you may well need to recruit at the level below, for which the next-best-thing may be ideal.

Analyse. Record. Do so against known criteria. Know in advance whether personality is more important than experience and where both rank against skills, knowledge, intelligence and willingness to do the job at the target salary. This implies that you know in advance when you are desperate, because there are few relevant applicants or the criteria are very tough. It will therefore permit you to decide while the candidate is present whether he or she may be the art of the possible and act accordingly, not necessarily by frightening them with an offer but by gathering up loose ends even more efficiently than usual and determining their reaction to a hypothetical package.

Bridge the Gap

In communication, particularly in and around the interview process, there is no such thing as a favourable variance. Messages, letters, offers, words heard, job descriptions, are never enhanced or made more intelligible by Acts of God or other means. Instead, they get corrupted, truncated, distorted in transmission (by people and machines), stray in the post, lost in the internal mail, on desks and in people's heads.

Worse, giving something precedence may even increase the chances it gets lost. The most important message or letter is often at the top of the pile – or the only one on the desk. It is therefore the one most likely to be picked up by static electricity and whisked away on the back of any plastic folder casually laid on top of it. We do not have an absolute cure for all of this, except to point out that if any interviewer wants to get the maximum out of any interview process he or she is totally responsible for ensuring that the communication line follows through to its ultimate destination and is understood. This means:

- always assuming a message has been lost unless a reply is received on time
- always trying to elicit a discriminating response to important messages, so you can verify transmission and receipt
- always making messages simple and self-contained (referring back to a previous document is not helpful if the addressee does not have it to hand)
- make it easy to reply by giving a clear indication what sort of response is needed, in what medium, with what degree of urgency. And *why*, if it is not very clear from the subject matter.

Something trivial may be on the Critical Path leading to a job offer, but if the candidate doesn't realize it is important it may be deferred; as a result, the offer is delayed and a competitive offer is not. The candidate is lost and the communication failure is to blame.

Always try to bridge the gap. Always consider what could go wrong and plan to avoid the problem.

Jargon

Interviewers often speak in the specialist jargon of their function, craft, trade or profession. This is tolerable if they are interviewing someone whose grasp of the jargon needs to be the equal of theirs as a requirement of the job, but it is wholly unproductive otherwise.

With all other interviewees, saying things in jargon ensures they are understood and remembered only as well as they might be if you said them in English to an Albanian peasant who stored them phonetically, if at all. At best it becomes a game of 'Chinese Whispers', in which even intelligent children inevitably distort any message as it proceeds from mouth to ear to brain to mouth to ear, and so on.

The symptoms are easy to observe. The hearer freezes and adopts a glazed expression, concentrating madly on the unknown word or phrase and, in the worst case, actually trying to remember it phonetically so that it can be researched later. The more decisive victims will allow it to flow through unremarked, but will still miss some of the message while deciding that the jargon cannot be decoded. The most assertive will actually pull the interviewer up and feign poor hearing or admit ignorance, but relatively few are brave enough.

Avoid the risk. Simplify your language. One way to do this is to imagine you are talking to a non-executive chairman who has just been appointed from a totally different sector. Nobody would want to risk offending him or her by a patronising flow of jargon. Extend an equal courtesy to the interviewees.

Past Indicative – Future Speculative

At this point it is comforting to retreat to the old principle that past behaviour is one of the best guides to future performance. This has the further merit that a review of past behaviour is based on events of which there may be a factual record. Tests and interviews which concentrate on a contemporary view of the individual – a snapshot approach, so to speak – suffer from the major disadvantage that one is working on opinions rather than facts. The same is true of any approach which works on the basis of the interviewee's answers to hypothetical questions. Any fool can give a textbook answer to the 'What would you do if . . .? sort of question, but they are likely to give a more informative response if the question relates back to something that actually happened. The answer is likely to be factual, or at least to have its roots in fact.

Perfection is unlikely. Those who froze or ran round in small circles screaming at the first sign of trouble will almost certainly find euphemisms for their behaviour but, short of these extremes, the past decision is likely to be mentioned, perhaps with a deprecatory indication that they would make a slightly more mature judgement now.

The key point is the link to fact. Given a free choice, facts are preferable to opinions. A good view of past facts is better than a better view of a contemporary opinion. All efforts which minimize reliance on opinions must be welcome. The sole exception is that a relevant formal test can be regarded as generating quasi-factual material, unlike interview results.

It is not unknown for a decisive interviewer to form an absolute judgement about an individual which is wholly at variance with the individual's past record (or future jobs). There is a dangerous willingness in interviewers, peer groups and bosses to extrapolate beyond a real or imagined weakness in a particular functional role and deduce incompetence in a wider role or a senior functional one, ignoring the fact that there is a bright side to the Peter Principle. You will recall that the Peter Principle postulates that people rise to their level of incompetence. The corollary is that many people appear incompetent when employed below their optimum level. Rather like bright children who are wrongly assessed at school because they are bored, someone can perform badly in a specialist functional job but be perfect for the more demanding one above.

The author has known several cases where opinionated managers have condemned subordinates as unfit for general management without even reading the victims' CVs, which clearly indicated successful past performance in such a role in equally demanding organizations.

As with so much criticism, the opinion tells you more about the critic than the subject of the comment. If this can happen in the work environment, how much more likely is a mistake in the truncated review possible during the interviews? Get the facts.

There is only one caveat, best expressed in the quotation 'The past is another country. They do things differently there.' At any rate, they *appear* to be doing things differently there, because observers often wear rose-coloured spectacles. Our insistence on facts from the past has to be coupled with a recognition that the facts will turn out somewhat pink in hindsight. However you can certainly allow for this.

Accentuate the Negative

Another classic interview problem is the interviewer who is obsessed with a desire to find out, in depressing detail, candidates' reasons for leaving all past jobs. It always tends to be a grey area . . . The tactic is to some extent acceptable, except that it invariably takes precedence over the more important business of finding out why the candidates joined their next employers. The focus on the negative ensures that interviewers omit, or do not thoroughly explore, the extremely encouraging reasons why people were dragged along to the next problem. There are four which we find quite attractive:

- they were genuinely headhunted, because their achievements were very visible
- a past employer wanted them back again
- an ex-boss pulled them on behind him or her to solve a known problem or complement an inadequate new team
- an ex-boss recommends them to his/her peers in a *different* company.

These factors are more compelling than references, interviews or some formal tests. We have *never* encountered a bad candidate who had been 'pulled through' in this way.

The Numerate Manager

Employers sometimes wonder why recruitment consultants, both in their paperwork and at interviews, place such an emphasis on numeracy. Actually, it isn't just numeracy, it's profit-orientation. Numerate managers know how many mickles make a muckle. For a start, they know that if some fathead spends £10,000 unnecessarily, someone else has to generate several times £10,000 in extra sales, just to break even . . .

Better still, they need people *in all functions of management* who realize that if your variable costs are 50 per cent of current sales revenue and overhead expenses 40 per cent, at current volumes, net profit before tax = 10 per cent of current sales revenue (assuming no bad debts) *and* there is thus a major profit opportunity if the company can improve sales (unit volume), prices, costs and overhead expenses by only 2½ per cent each.

sales revenues go up to		105.06 (half due to price, half to volume)	
variable costs go down			
would have been	51.25		
less 2½%	1.28 =	49.97	55.09
and overheads fall back to			39.00
leaving net profit at			16.09

An improvement of **60%** at the bottom line!

Managers who understand this and work toward it are very popular. That's why we keep trying to find them!

Honesty is the Best Policy

Far too many otherwise reasonable interviewers close an
interview without indicating to the victims that they have made
a decision – and why. Sometimes this is necessary. More often,
it is merely a question of trying to be nice and to run an
inoffensive event which causes the least emotional damage – to
the interviewer, that is.

The author would like to make a plea for disclosure. There
are several reasons. The first is that, properly done, it must
improve communication. Second, it may actually be less
stressful for both parties. Third, it may allow for the correction
of errors or omissions.

Let us take specific examples. If you are rejecting someone,
for the right reasons (like a mismatch with the candidate
specification or the fact that they meet it substantially less well
than people you have already met who are actively interested
and available at your price), you end their period of uncertainty
and avoid or reduce the possibility they will think a future cold
written rejection is because they performed badly in other
respects. It also gives you the chance to say face to face that
you like them and, if true, that you would like to have them
on the team at some future date in another job.

If you are considering making an offer, it keeps their interest and
permits a preliminary discussion about the package they would find
acceptable – if later candidates do not displace them! A clear
declaration of intent at this stage entitles you to enquire about their
interest with more authority, and about the competition.

If you are rejecting them for the wrong reasons, like a
shortage of specific experience, being open about it gives the
candidates a chance to correct any omissions. This may not drag
them back into first place, but it clears the air and improves
the chances that the meeting was not wasted. Both of you can
feel that honour was satisfied and the candidates will feel they
had a fair chance.

Prompt rejection brings other bonuses. You don't have to
write a later letter, except as a grace note. You don't risk
forgetting to do so. You don't risk forgetting your decision, or
the reasons for it. You have saved your time and theirs.

CONCLUSION

By this time readers will have realized the essentially schizophrenic nature of this book. On the one hand, it recognizes the objective criticism that conventional interviews are hopelessly inadequate as a predictor of work performance, so much of the book is devoted to complementary methods of assessment On the other hand, we have to recognize that the conventional interview is not going to curl up and vanish just because a number of experts criticize it, so attention has to be given to improving this very imperfect tool.

There are a few crumbs of comfort buried in the text, however. In particular, when next immersed in the sort of interview that makes you wish they could be abolished, console yourself with the thought that even if the interview isn't too hot as a predictor of work performance, it has several other roles. A thorough interviewer can use them, for example, to gather, amplify and analyse data about the individual's current state and past behaviour. Both are important factors in any assessment process. They can also be used to review and discuss the results of formal tests, are a valid arena for exploring communication skills and, properly planned, may permit you to explore people's considered reactions to specific work problems. They also permit a future boss and employee to decide whether they can tolerate one another. Not wholly objective, but necessary.

The other thing which is going to keep the interview alive for quite a few years yet is peer-group pressure. Even if you convince yourself that the recruitment interview is redundant, colleagues are going to be incredulous when they realize that you hire without interviewing and positively scornful when the first unsatisfactory result of that process is identified. It will not help to point to the dozens of less than satisfactory people they have hired with the 'aid' of interviews. Prejudice knows no logic. It follows that you are stuck with the darn things. Make the best of it.

Further best-selling management books from IPM

20 Ways to Manage Better
Andrew Leigh

An invaluable distillation of management wisdom which deserves a place on every manager's desk.

The book has 20 short chapters, each on a different topic, which the busy manager can use to improve his or her performance. They include: setting objectives, coaching, problem people, controlling your time, meetings, negotiating, better reading and listening, recruitment and selection.

'The author grabs your attention at the opening of each chapter and whisks you through to the closing sentence quite painlessly. But en route he has given you plenty to think about, and more importantly, plenty to put into operation in your office tomorrow.'
The Director
0 85292 334 1

Management Methods
Derek Torrington, Jane Weightman and Kirsty Johns

Management Methods is a handbook for the busy manager who doesn't have time to read many management books. It follows a unique 'dip-in' format with 50 action plans covering many different situations and concise explanations of why the relevant methods should work, as well as how to work them. The plans deal with a wide range of management activities, from report-writing to organizational politics, from the subtleties of counselling to the precision of statistical sampling. All the units are self-contained, making the book especially convenient to browse through on trains, at airports, at home, or to use when preparing for a meeting.

'a really useful book, the sort of book you would actually wish to buy and have with you when doing things.'
The Times Higher Educational Supplement
0 85292 355 4

Everyone Needs a Mentor
How to foster talent within the organization
David Clutterbuck

Mentoring promises to be the management development technique of the future. Generations of new young employees have learned the company ropes, developed their experience and confidence and progressed up the career ladder under the watchful guidance of more experienced managers. The well-known writer and journalist, David Clutterbuck explains the formalization of this process and explores all aspects of mentoring.

'Anyone involved in training and staff development cannot afford to ignore this innovative means of fostering talent.'
Management Services

0 85292 345 7

Staff Appraisal
A first step to effective leadership
Gerry Randell, Peter Packard and John Slater

This completely revised and updated edition presents an analytical approach to the skills of staff appraisal and advocates training techniques to improve managers' ability to monitor their subordinates' performance and develop their potential.

The book successfully combines academic analysis with industrial relevance to produce an extremely readable book for all those who want to improve their management and leadership skills.

0 85292 333 3

Creating a Committed Workforce
Peter Martin and John Nicholls

Learn the lessons of the British success stories of the 1980s!

How have major companies achieved dramatic improvements in productivity and results? In this perceptive and hard hitting study, the authors go behind the scenes and talk to the leaders in 14 pioneering businesses like Jaguar and Raleigh, Burton and Schweppes. Here they find profound changes – such as profit-sharing, systematic disclosure of information, flatter management structures, worker accountability for quality and moves towards 'single status' – are commonplace. Such changes reflect the impact of Japanese and American management; they are also laying the foundations for the resurgence of UK industry and commerce.

0 85292 379 1

The Institute of Personnel Management is one of the leading publishers of books for personnel professionals, general managers and students. For further information on the full range of IPM titles please contact

The Publications Department
The Institute of Personnel Management
IPM House
Camp Road
London SW19 4UW
Tel: (01) 946 9100